Praise for

Fishing on the Edge

"A fascinating look behind the scenes of professional bass fishing. In addition, it goes beyond the flash and hype to show off Iaconelli's real talent as a serious angler, providing how-to chapters that'll help the reader become a better bass angler."—*Burlington (VT) Free Press*

"An honest, behind-the-scenes look at life as a bass angling pro."
—*Herald Democrat*

"Ike does bare enough of his soul to touch something greater. . . . We get a glimpse inside the tours [and] there's enough dirt that dirt-seekers won't walk away too disappointed."—Bassfan.com

"Like [Iaconelli] the book is rowdy, blunt. . . . It's also fun, and chock-full of fishing info and cool lists."—*Philadelphia Inquirer*

"Entertaining . . . It's a great read and something every sports fan should get their hands on."—midamericaoutdoors.com

"A candid look into the life of a talented, ultra-meticulous professional bass angler. Iaconelli's autobiography portrays a champion of his age."—*Arkansas Democrat-Gazette*

Fishing

ON THE
EDGE

Mike Iaconelli

WITH

Andrew and Brian Kamenetzky

FISHING ON THE EDGE
A Delta Book

PUBLISHING HISTORY
Delacorte Press hardcover edition published May 2005
Delta trade paperback edition / June 2006

Published by
Bantam Dell
A Division of Random House, Inc.
New York, New York

Book design by Susan Hood

Library of Congress Catalog Card Number: 2005047020
Delta is a registered trademark of Random House, Inc., and the colophon is a
trademark of Random House, Inc.

ISBN-10: 0-385-34008-7
ISBN-13: 978-0-385-34008-3

Printed in the United States of America
Published simultaneously in Canada

www.bantamdell.com

BVG 10 9 8 7 6 5

THIS BOOK is dedicated to my family. Thanks Mom, Uncle Don, Gram, and Pop for helping me become the man I am today. Because of you, I've been able to turn my childhood hobby and passion into a fulltime dream job. You always believed in me and gave me the confidence that I could do anything in life I wanted to. And to my two girls, Drew and Rylie. I love you more than anything in this world. Follow your heart and strive to achieve your dreams. And remember, never give up!

Fishing
ON THE **EDGE**

THE BREAKING POINT

Everyone has his passion. His calling. His purpose in life. For as long as I can remember, mine has always been fishing. Nothing except the love of my family has ever given me more joy. The art of finding and landing fish. Beating them in *their* environment. From the moment I dropped a line into the water as a toddler, everything in my life had been steered down a single path: making a living as a professional bass fisherman. In 1999, after years of grinding it out on the amateur level, my dream became a reality. I filed the paperwork with BASS (Bass Anglers Sportsman Society), the grand-daddy of bass fishing tournament organizations, and jumped into the fire. Almost immediately, I won the Vermont BASS Top 150 Pro Tour on Lake Champlain, beating fishing legend (and my hero) Rick Clunn by almost two pounds. Even better than pocketing $100,000, more money than I had ever seen at once in my life, I knew I had arrived, that I was really and truly living my dream. I was on top of the world, and thought I'd stay there forever.

Fast-forward to March 2003. The high was long gone and I had be-come a mental train wreck. I was toast! Fried! Why? My marriage was over, and that was all I could think about. I was sleeping no more than two hours a night, I couldn't eat, and I couldn't sleep. Even worse, it felt like fishing was the reason my marriage had crumbled. Being a profes-sional angler is a huge time commitment. All of that attention put towards fishing had always been a sore spot between me and my soon-to-be-ex-wife, Kristi. My travel demands meant I was away from her and my daughters, Drew and Rylie, for days, weeks, sometimes months on end. Even when I was home, I had to spend time on research, and main-taining and preparing my gear. I've always said that dedication and hard work, not natural talent, allowed me to succeed, so I never allowed my-self to let up for one second. That created even more distance between me and Kristi. Everything had come to a head and our relationship had, sadly, reached the breaking point.

A time line of mistakes, consequences, and guilt kept racing through my mind. I told myself, "If you were a normal Joe, none of this would have happened. . . . You wanted it all. . . . You just *had* to be a profes-sional angler!" It felt like every bad thing that had happened to me was because of fishing. Of course, I was ignoring the zillions of positives, which had always outweighed the bad, but by now my mind was Swiss cheese. I decided I had to make some radical changes in my life. Salvaging my marriage wasn't even the issue. I knew Kristi and I were getting divorced. But I couldn't go through this kind of pain again. I had to give myself a normal life so I wouldn't ruin my next relationship. After months of thinking it over, I finally came to a decision I never thought I'd make.

I'd quit fishing for good.

I was dead serious. I was gone. Out. I had made up my mind, and anyone who knows me will tell you that when my mind's made up, there's no changing it. My family knew that, so when I told them, they asked me only one simple question—"Are you sure?" Fishing had been my number one passion my whole life, so they wanted to be certain I had thought through what it meant to quit, but I was too depressed for sensible meditation. Fishing had wrecked my personal life, and I wanted out. It happens to tons of anglers. Pete Gluszek, my best friend and roommate on tour, had watched relationships with his ex-wife and a recent girlfriend land in the toilet. For many guys, that's the unfortunate reality of the sport. But I always thought Kristi and I were different, that we'd be the exception to the rule.

Try to picture this, though: I'd never experienced life without fishing being front and center. In my first memories, I have a rod in my hands. As a kid, my summers revolved around trips to the Poconos, where I caught trout, sunfish, and, eventually, my first bass. I collected *Bassmaster* magazines the way most kids collected baseball cards. After I graduated from Triton High School in Runnemede, New Jersey, I was more concerned about starting my fishing club, Top Rod Bassmasters, than enrolling in college. When I eventually earned my degree, I had done it by cramming for tests in between fishing pro-am tournaments. It didn't matter what I was doing, or where life had taken me. Fishing always found its place in the mix. I couldn't imagine it any other way.

Plus, I was living the life most fishermen would kill for. My career earnings were well into six figures. I was being sponsored by some of the biggest names in the business. Ranger Boats. Yamaha (outboard motors). Team Daiwa (rods and reels). Stren (fishing line). Owner (hooks). Fitovers Eyewear. Mann's Bait Company. Dick's Sporting Goods. You could count the number of years I'd been a pro on one hand and still have a finger left over, yet I'd already won three times on the BASS tour. Some guys fish as a pro for twenty years without winning even one. After years of scratching and clawing, I had made it. Yet there I was, ready to go back to my old job running the fishing department at Dick's

Sporting Goods in Mount Laurel, New Jersey, while I completed a post-baccalaureate teaching program at Rowan University. I'd already ordered the paperwork for school. I'd moved on. That seemed like the only answer to my problems.

But I still had a grand vision. I didn't want to just crawl away from the sport that I'd loved so much and had shaped my life. I wanted to go out in style, and there was no better way than winning the last tournament I'd ever fish: the 2003 Citgo Bassmaster Classic, down in the Louisiana Delta near New Orleans. The Bassmaster Classic has always been the Super Bowl of bass fishing. No event even comes close, so it was the perfect send-off. This wasn't about nostalgia, though. I was no Ray Bourque, who played twenty-one seasons in the NHL before finally winning a Stanley Cup in 2001 and going out a champ. Give me a break! Fishing had turned its back on me and robbed me blind, so I wanted to squeeze every last drop I could from it. I was going to grab this title and then tell the entire sport to kiss off!

When June rolled around, which was a month before the Classic, I drove to the Big Easy with my uncle Don for the official six-day practice period. To me, this research and preparation time, during which I would break down the five hundred thousand fishable acres of the Delta and settle on a strategy, would make or break my entire tournament. Once those six days were over, anglers wouldn't be allowed near the tournament waters until the event started. So I needed to make each one count. Unfortunately, by the fifth day, I felt absolutely defeated because I wasn't anywhere near the fish.

It was frustrating, because even though I was quitting afterward, I had done the same homework for this tournament that I would for any other. I pored over maps and did hours upon hours of Internet research. I scoured my old *Bassmaster* magazines for useful tips. I scooped up information anywhere I could find it, so I felt too well prepared for such bad results. (Obviously, since I was working so hard, I should have realized that deep down I still loved the sport. This wasn't the most rational period in my life.) And on top of everything, I knew the Delta well. My first Classic, in 1999, was on the same fishery, and I'd finished sixth. And that was before I'd even officially turned pro!

But after spending two days working spots around an area called Bayou Black, where I'd hauled fifteen pounds in '99, I'd barely landed any weight at all. Each day we're allowed to catch a limit of five fish. At no point can we have more than five fish in our live well. If we pull in a sixth, we have to toss one back. Well, I had managed to catch a limit, but it was a pathetic six pounds. You think six pounds a day will win the Classic? Think again. On my third day of practice, I moved to a completely different area of the Delta called Venice and had a little more success, but the next day I mismanaged my time on the water and lost any momentum I had going. Four days had passed, two were left, and I still hadn't found that winning spot.

So on Day Five, I decided to fish an area called Delta Duck (you gotta love the names of these places!). This was a last-ditch effort. I was pulling the cord on the emergency parachute. If it didn't work, I'd have to go back to Old Dennis for my last practice day, learn it like the back of my hand, and pray for the best. I reached the Duck, and just like every other day that week, the morning just sucked. By one o'clock I had caught only one good fish and one little keeper. Terrible. I thought about bailing, even though I knew the time I'd spend traveling to my next spot would basically waste the day. I had made that same stupid mistake just the day before. The only thing grayer than my mood was the sky, and before I could even ask my uncle his opinion, the clouds puked up an ugly storm. Rain and lightning poured relentlessly from a thick, menacing sky. It was literally terrifying to watch. I looked around, but there was nowhere to hide. The Duck, like the rest of the Delta, is just marsh, reeds, and water. No protection anywhere.

We couldn't outrun the storm. All we could do was jam the boat into the reeds to create a primitive canopy. Gee, great! Now we weren't getting *as* soaked. I curled up pathetically on the front of the deck, which had the most "protection." I lay there, miserable, cold, and depressed, with all of my life's disasters running through my head, pushing me toward a nervous breakdown. I was at rock bottom. Which makes what happened next even more bizarre.

I fell asleep.

It was the weirdest thing that's happened to me in my entire career. I'd never slept on my boat while I was on the water. Ever. But there I was, drifting off despite all the noise in my head and the weather beating down on me. But there was one thing I knew for sure, which was a great source of comfort. This horrible chapter in my life as a fisherman was nearly over.

I just didn't know a new one was about to start.

1 IN THE BEGINNING

Anglers everywhere treat the opening day of trout season like a religious event. It's no different in Philadelphia, except the fishing gets so dicey afterward you'd better catch them while you can. So it would be no surprise to see my family kicking off trout season at the Wissahickon Creek, a branch of the Delaware River outside the city. I stood on the bank and dropped a line with a piece of corn on the end into the water. When this little trout chomped down on the kernel, I pulled the fish out. A huge grin crossed my face, and I was so excited I probably wet myself. But at least I had an excuse.

I was still in diapers.

That was the first fish I caught, and the last time any fish could rest easy. I was almost two years old.

Mike and the Family Ike

I was born on June 17, 1972. My first memories of home begin at our three-story row house in South Philadelphia, where I lived with my mom, Roberta, my uncle Don, my grandfather Joseph (who I called Pop), and my grandmom Edith. Even though I was little, I vividly remember that house, especially the tiny backyard. It was only twenty by eighteen feet, and nearly concreted over, but Pop and Grandmom still managed to grow a garden back there in the cement, housing an awesome assortment of vegetables, as well as the box turtles we used to keep as pets. Inside, I can remember huge rooms with tons of space. Maybe they just seemed big to me at the time. I'm not sure.

Technically, my first home was an apartment on Broad Street with my mom, and, I'm assuming, my dad. Unfortunately, he passed away around the same time I caught that first fish. I don't have any memories of my father—I've never even seen a picture of him. My mom has never shown me any, and I've never asked to see one. Maybe it's because we've maintained no relationship with his side of the family. He's not a subject I've ever really pressed my mom about. I've always felt that if there was anything really important I should know, she would tell me. Apparently, we look alike and share the same outgoing personality. One other thing I do know: he didn't fish.

Despite growing up without a father, I never felt a void, because Pop and Uncle Don quickly became father figures to me. My mom's side of the family was always super close, and from day one they've supported anything and everything I've done. It's because of them that I've become the angler, and the person, I am today.

Fishing and the outdoors run through my family's blood. My great-grandfather, Grandmom's dad, never lost his love of fishing despite being stuck in the city. Every day, he threw a line in the Schuylkill River, another tributary of the Delaware that nearly runs through downtown Philly. Pop was also hooked on fishing, and after he grew up and had my mom, Don, Aunt Joanne, and Uncle Joe, he took them every year to the Jersey Shore and the Poconos. This tradition continued after I was born and would be key to my development as an angler.

On to Jersey

My mom's family has deep roots in South Philly. Pop was born in the house his mother lived in, next door to the house where his kids grew up. Aunts and cousins lived down the street. When my mom was a kid, you didn't have to lock your doors, neighbors looked out for each other, and kids could play kickball or stickball in the street. But by the time I was born, the area had started turning. Now you had to worry about getting beat up on the way to school or going to the store for groceries. My uncle has told me stories, and they're no fun. I can't imagine growing up in that kind of environment. Fortunately, I didn't have to.

By the time I entered kindergarten, my family, especially my mom, had had enough. It was time to go. My starting school gave them a good excuse to leave, but in reality they were always outdoors people who hated being tied to the city. So the whole family unit—Mom, Don, Pop, Grandmom, and me—moved to Runnemede, New Jersey, the heart of suburbia. Even though we were only about twenty-five minutes outside Philly, it felt like we had moved to another planet. We had a double lot on the corner, almost an entire acre. I had gone from a tiny concrete back-yard to a huge expanse of grass and trees, which was amazing. Soon, Pop started a new garden, with tomatoes, corn, and cabbage quickly swallowing up one quarter of the property. I remember the sense of pride they felt after moving out to the suburbs. They'd been working their whole lives to get there. It was like, "We did it. We're living in the good neighborhood now."

2 UP IN THE POCONOS

Most of my early memories of South Philly are like still pictures, just images and flashes. My first real recollections are from the Poconos, where we'd take family trips at the beginning and the end of every summer. I don't quite remember my first, when I was still an infant, but I remember most of the ones afterward. I can still close my eyes and remember the three cabins—cabin 1, cabin 2, and cabin 3—right on the shore of Fairview Lake. Each had two to four bedrooms, a kitchen, and a porch. They were built perpendicular to the lakefront with a T-dock extending into the water. Cabin 1, right on the lake, was Pop's favorite, not because it was the biggest, but because it was the closest to the water. He always slept in the front room with the big window. "Pop's room" was off limits to everyone else . . . except Grandmom, of course.

Fishing was a big part of the trip, but there were a lot of other highlights, too. It was about the whole outdoor experience. There were water sports and swimming. We'd walk to this tiny rock-quarry pond and I'd catch these cool-looking water salamanders that I'd take home and keep as pets (they'd always die). At night, we would get ice cream at an old-fashioned country store or go into Hawley, the nearest town, to watch drive-in movies and eat at the hot dog stand. It was a different deal from even suburban New Jersey, right out of a Norman Rockwell painting. It was something everyone looked forward to. Looking back, I didn't realize what an escape the trips were for my family. They worked hard all year for those two weeks in the summer.

Learning to Fish

When I first started, everything was really basic. I used the same simple spin-cast equipment my grandfather and uncle used. A five-foot rod with a closed face and push-button release reel. My earliest memories aren't of being on the water, but of fishing off the dock. Pop or Don would sometimes just get a stick, tie a line with a hook and bait on the end, and drop it in. We'd catch 'em almost every time. Bluegill, trout, and other panfish, with a stick! But in those early days, no matter what I used for a rod, the bait was always live, mostly worms, night crawlers, mealworms, and corn. (I know the last one sounds stupid, but stocked trout love kernel corn. I don't write the menu, you know?) I don't think my uncle even owned any lures. Pop had a few, but the only time we used them was while trolling from spot to spot, just dragging the lure behind the boat before finding an area to still-fish.

Captain Pop

Sometimes the whole family would cast off the dock, but the boat trips with me, Don, and Pop dominate my fishing memories in the Poconos. We'd be out on our little johnboat, always with my uncle in back, me in the middle, and Pop in front. In the beginning, Don had to sit back there and row because we didn't have a trolling motor. Fairview Lake wasn't huge, maybe ninety acres, but still, that's a lot of rowing! Plus, Pop would always tease Don, bugging him to row faster. "Put a little oomph in it, Don!" When we finally got our first electric trolling motor, this sad little green box with maybe ten pounds of thrust, it hardly moved the boat, but we—and by *we* I mean my uncle—thought it rocked, because at least it meant the end of manual labor. Plus, I occasionally got to steer using the trolling motor, which was *huge* for me.

I remember my grandfather and uncle being really into fishing strategically. Picking the right cast for the right situation. Deciding to pull the bait off the bottom by six inches instead of a foot. How to properly set the hook. They were trying to figure out the fish, which was a huge influence on me as my skills developed. Between solving mysteries, we'd just shoot the breeze. Don's relationship with Pop was a lot like *Sanford and Son*, only with white guys. They'd get into little scuffles when stuff would go wrong, or Don wasn't paddling fast enough. Nothing serious, just a dad giving his son a hard time, always with a playful wink. It was hilarious, because my grandfather was always *the man*, especially out on the water. It was his way or no way, you know? Even when Pop was wrong, he was right. Those times were absolutely the best.

Testing the Boundaries

Even on those early trips when I was still a couple of years away from getting hooked into fishing just for bass, I used to suck up information and technique. Pop and Don were great teachers, helping me cast, instructing me about angles. But the biggest lesson they taught me was patience. When I saw that bite, I'd automatically want to start reeling in. But there's an art to landing a fish. Waiting until it has the bait, and then setting the hook. Set too early, and the fish won't be securely hooked. Of all the skills Pop and Don coached me on, patience was the most important.

But even as a little kid, I'd push the limits of my skill. We fished for trout back then, which is angling at its most basic. But whenever we met other fishermen in the Poconos or back in New Jersey, I always watched what they did and asked questions. Then I would take that information back out on the water. Before I knew it, I started stepping above my uncle and my grandfather, observing conditions and making adjustments. Replacing a gold swivel with a black one because the brightness made the fish skittish, swapping out my line types, and eventually going to better hooks. Refining the whole art of trout fishing.

Every time Pop watched me change my line or my swivel, he was totally skeptical, always growling, "Aw, that ain't gonna make a difference." It was hilarious how he used to bust my chops. Then I started catching some big numbers. As my results got better, my uncle eventually caught on and followed suit, getting into the spinning equipment and artificial bait I used. But Pop never changed equipment or technique. He defined the old-school fisherman. I don't care if you had a magic lure guaranteed to pull fifteen-inch trout out every time—he wouldn't put it on his line. He always scoffed, "Aw, I don't need that!" And it was true. He didn't. My grandfather was a natural. Even with the junk he used, never taking advantage of any new technology, he could still match our catches. It was pretty impressive.

Pop and Don never got upset when I started outcatching them. In fact, it was the opposite. They were really proud at how good I was getting. But while my family slowly became accustomed to me bringing in big stringers, it always kind of freaked other people out. Whether it was out on Wissahickon Creek in my diapers, or on the T-dock before I was in kindergarten, people were always shocked and impressed. During one of our Poconos trips when I was about ten, my mom and I rented a boat on a little lake called Peck's Pond. It was a full house on the water, but nobody was catching anything . . . except this goofy elementary-school kid who landed a limit. When I got back to the dock, I remember one dude looking at my stringer and blurting out a curse word or two. So much for keeping it clean around the kid, you know?

GO WITH YOUR GUT

Fishing is pure form and function. All that matters is getting fish into the boat. *How* is up to you. Too often, though, anglers are reluctant to try anything weird or unconventional. Obviously, I don't have that problem, and it usually pays off. Here are three ways to take your fishing out of the box.

CASTING. I use seven basic casts on any bank or stretch of open water: a flip, a pitch, an overhead (your basic long cast), a sidearm roll, an overhand roll, a straight skip, and a pitch skip. (I don't take total credit, but I like to think of "pitch skip" as a cast I helped introduce and perfect.) Pretend your living room is a fishery. A flip may sneak a worm between the fireplace and window, but an overhand roll's better for slipping a spinnerbait under the coffee table. To slide your Stone Jig under the ottoman, maybe the pitch skip is best. Same idea on the water. Every tiny crack between a sailboat, a dock post, or an overhanging tree is different, and requires a different strategy. Don't fear a "tripping on acid" cast that combines everything you know and a little luck. I'd cast with my feet if I thought it would work.

THE IMPOSSIBLE CAST. During my first major win on Lake Champlain, in '99, I was catching fish by pitching my jig inside rows of tires set up as wave breaks (obstacles that cut wave action near a marina), sometimes bouncing them off other rows as I reeled them in. Obviously, this wasn't a high-percentage cast, but at the same time, I always want the opportunity to catch every fish. Just the opportunity! Ninety percent of anglers wouldn't cast into tires because it's an "impossible" cast. It's not! The only "impossible" cast is the one you don't make. Get it?

LURES. During my club days, I found myself trying to skip little four-inch plastic worms on light line under docks using spinning equipment, but kept breaking off my line on the obstacles, or because the fish were too big. So my friend John McGraw and I created a jig head that reached deep-cover spots using heavy line and conventional equipment. We found a walleye head with a flat surface and tweaked the design until we got it right. We called it a Stone Jig, and this lure that was once poured in my grandmom's basement now sells by the thousands yearly for Mann's Bait Company. Do you have to invent lures to make an impact? No. But don't be afraid to tweak. Dip 'em in dyes, trim baits, or file them down. If you think a plastic crab imitation will work better than the jig everyone's throwing, do it and learn from the results. Regardless of what you catch, you'll end up a better angler.

3
CATCHING "THE ONE"

By the time I was twelve, I had been fishing trout in the Poconos with my family for over ten years. I'd caught a few bass up to that point, but they were little. A fingerling (a couple of inches long) to maybe half a foot, tops. And I had never caught one on purpose. The only time I even used artificial baits was trolling around, usually with basic inline spinners. So heading up to the lake that June, I was just looking forward to another week of catching trout and having fun. I had no idea my life was about to change.

Pop's Box

Pop had a great tackle box, a hip, roof-style green Coleman with a brass latch that opened in three tiers, with a built-in ruler inside. At the time, it was state of the art, and held hooks, weights, line, swivels, mineral oil, everything. And the smell was incredible, you know? All musty, old, and watery. I had been in awe of it since I was little. This was *Pop's box*, the Holy Grail of tackle boxes. He'd open it and light would pour out, the angels would sing, and I'd bow down. All hail the Coleman!

More than anything, I was mesmerized by his small collection of lures (even today, building up my collection of cool lures is part of the sport's appeal). I can still remember every lure in there, some of the most old-school stuff ever sold, bait you'd see now and say, "What is this stuff?" He had these spinners called CP Swings, a basic in-line spinner. There were old Cream baits, tiny rubber imitations of a cricket or a frog. He even had red-and-white Daredevil spoons, silver-backed, spoon-shaped metal slabs with a picture of a devil in the center. The only other artificial lure he had was a Rapala, basically a floating minnow bait with a small lip on the end.

Pop was incredibly protective of his tackle box. He'd see me looking around in it and snap, "What are you doing in there? Stay out of my box!" Again, always with his little smile. Pop was Fred Sanford, all bark and no bite. But at ten or eleven years old, even Fred Sanford was enough to keep me out of the Coleman.

Crossing the Line

The first morning of that summer's trip to the Poconos, I hit the dock to cast a few before Pop and Uncle Don came out. It was just gonna be another day of trout fishing, but today, Pop's box kept calling my name. Maybe it was the excitement of being back at the lake, but I couldn't resist going in and grabbing something to throw off the dock. I pulled out a 9S Floating Rapala—black on the back, silver sides, two treble hooks: one on the belly, one on the tail. At the time, I didn't even know what it was. I just reached into the Coleman and pulled it out.

The scene is still vivid in my mind. I'm out on the end of the T-dock, there's a little fog on the lake, and the water is slick and calm. My rod was still rigged to catch panfish and trout, which meant line out of the reel attached to a swivel, a snelled hook, and a Water Gremlin split shot.

So I pinched the ears of the Gremlin, popped it off, removed the snelled hook, and attached the Rapala, with absolutely no idea how to fish it or what it was going to do in the water. All I knew how to do was cast, which by now I did pretty well. I threw out the Rapala in a big, beautiful arc, ripples moving away as it hit the water. It just floated there. That's what it was supposed to do, but I didn't know.

For the first few seconds, I just stared at this strange, floating bait. Then I gave the reel four or five cranks, watching the Rapala's swimming action. I was astonished. I'd never seen a lure behave like that. And as I thought, "Okay, it's a bait you cast, swim, and reel in," the bait floated back to the surface, where I let it sit for another couple of seconds. *Whoosh!* This bass—not a giant, but at almost three pounds it was the biggest fish I'd ever seen— blew out of the water, mouth wide open, swallowing the Rapala. The visual was the most intense thing I'd ever seen. In trout fishing, you drag live bait along the bottom of the water, watching your rod tip or bobber. I had never seen a fish explode out of the water after a lure. I don't even think I set the hook! If the bass hadn't totally engulfed that lure, I probably wouldn't have brought it in.

I could barely breathe as I used every ounce of energy to land that fish. It gave me a fight like I'd never experienced, bulldogging me and splashing all the way back to the dock. I was flipping out, thinking, "If that line breaks, I'm gonna have to fess up to taking the lure, *and* replace it . . . *And nobody's gonna believe I caught it to begin with!*" It was a situation where I had to beat that fish, the first of many over the course of my career.

Why Don't You Just Keep That Thing?

Once I had it on the dock, I started screaming bloody murder, running back to cabin 3, where we were staying that year. I didn't even know how to hold a bass back then, so I just ran with the fish hanging off the end of my line. "Aaaaaaaggggghhh!" My family must have thought I was being stabbed to death by some lakeside killer. I busted through the door, the bass dangling off my rod tip like a hanging grenade, and everybody freaked. Pop thought it was the biggest fish in the world. And not being a catch-and-release guy, the first thing out of his mouth was "Get my stringer! Put him on the stringer!" My new buddy was getting some Crisco and breading that night. By now, Pop knew I had raided his box, but he was too proud to care. In fact, he gave me the bait, saying, "Why don't you just go ahead and keep using that thing." I had gone from "never go in there and touch that" to throwing this awesome Rapala lure whenever I pleased.

PANIC BOX

Fishing gets tough for a lot of reasons. A cold front hits. Increased boat pressure from weekend anglers. Maybe the fish have seen too much of what you're throwing. Whatever the reason, even pros have days when primary and secondary patterns fail, and nothing's working. I've actually stocked a Plano 3600 box, literally labeled PANIC BOX, specifically for this situation. Inside are all my finesse baits, the smaller lures, weights, and lines I used as a kid to catch trout, panfish, and anything else that swims. The panic box has bailed me out so many times, it's scary. That's why it never leaves my boat.

When it hits the fan, I immediately grab my favorite "hard times" bait, a Berkley 4-inch Power Finesse Worm. Basic in shape and naturally colored, it might be the most versatile worm ever. I'll often tie on a small split shot in lean situations, allowing me to fish heavier cover, throw a Texas rig-style presentation or even a drop shot. These work best if I'd previously caught them on bottom running a Carolina rig or Stone Jig.

If I'd been slow-rolling spinnerbaits or crankbaiting, I might bust a grub, specifically a 3-inch model, either curly tailed (Berkley Power Grub) or straight (Sting Ray), depending on the environmental conditions. Back in my Federation days, I was fishing a spot on the Potomac River called Arkendale Flats and was crushing 'em with two of the standard power-fishing lures, Carolina rigs and rattletraps. But the flat got beat up bad by boat traffic (mine included), a cold front rolled in overnight, and the fish stopped biting. After switching to a small, white, curly-tailed grub and using smaller-scale crankbait tactics, I caught a limit on a day when a lot of guys struck out.

Be prepared to take guff from your buddies if you break out my next panic lure—an old fashioned in-line spinner. When the spinnerbaits are burned out, or the bass are simply ignoring topwater lures, use a gold or silver spinner, maybe even a chartreuse in-line spinner with a willow or Indiana blade. I'll even use hair jigs, with some kind of pork trailer (an additional lure attached to the bait, made from real pigskin), in colder water when Stone Jigs or jigging spoons fail. I throw three basic colors, brown, black, and gray/white, 1/16 to 1/4 ounce, and favor deer hair.

Desperate times call for desperate measures. Don't be afraid to go old school when conditions dictate. And remember to adjust your rod and line to use panic lures effectively. Lighter lures mean lighter line. Then slow down. You can't cover the same amount of water, and the heavier cover will cause some trouble. Finally, lower your expectations. Smaller baits mean smaller fish. Will you win a tournament on panic lures? Probably not. But while my limit on Arkendale Flats wasn't huge, it landed me in the top six, which qualified me for regionals, which got me into the Federation nationals, where my win took me to the '99 Classic. Moral of the story? Every fish counts.

Hooked on Bass

After that day, I couldn't think about anything but catching more bass. That was a breakthrough point, not just because it hooked me on bass fishing, but also because it changed me as an angler. Later that morning, I felt antsy sitting and still-fishing, waiting for the trout to bite. Just sitting . . . and waiting. I wanted to be throwing and moving, seeing that bass torpedo out of the water. I had already started developing what would become my power-fishing style, where I'm constantly moving not only my body but also the lure in the water, working it fast and hard.

I didn't catch any more bass that trip, but I returned to Runnemede obsessed with getting that next one. I wanted to learn more. I told my friends the story, and they were psyched. They started taking a bigger interest in bass fishing. That summer, my buddy Tom Hrynyshyn gave me one of his dad's old *Bassmaster* magazines. It was the February 1985 issue, and the cover was a bass being caught on a 11G floating Rapala. I saved it, and just about every *Bassmaster* magazine that has been produced since. (I still have them cataloged at my uncle's place in Runnemede.) Soon afterward, my buddies and I started playing with the Rapala on Stewart Lake and other local fisheries, learning its strengths and weaknesses. Each day I got more excited catching bass, each new experience feeding on the one before.

Bass on the Brain

But it really wasn't until I returned to the Poconos the following June that I became hard-core obsessed with bass fishing. That first day back, I didn't even wait for my family to unpack before I ran to the dock. I tossed that same Rapala into a couple of patches of lily pads, and caught three in a row. Boom! Boom! Boom! The third was a five-pounder, a massive beast! It looked like Jaws coming out of the water.

If I wasn't completely hooked before, I was now!

When I took Jaws back to the cabin, instead of being eaten, he was wrapped in a towel and put in the freezer. When we got back to Jersey, Pop, Don, and I took it to Ribbs Taxidermy for stuffing. It cost something like ten dollars an inch. We had no idea it was that expensive! We're talking about a 20-inch fish! But Pop was so psyched he gladly paid the bill, then stuck the fish on the living room wall of his house in Runnemede. I think it's still there.

Evolution of a Bass Fisherman

Reading that *Bassmaster* magazine that Tom Hrynyshyn gave me, I was enthralled by every page of colorful, shiny baits. I used all my chore, Christmas, and birthday money to build my collection. I became more conscious about my equipment, line, tackle, and technique in general. In the beginning, I was using only that Rapala and a few in-line spinners, but I knew I wanted to expand my horizons. It wasn't anything premeditated, but every year I learned a new lure, spending the whole season trying to master it. I'd explore it on top, swimming it, learning where it was good and where it wasn't. After working the Rapala to death, I spent the following winter reading about plastic curly-tailed grubs. That summer, everything was about the grub. Then tubes, then plastic worms, then spinnerbaits, then jigs. I spent each year concentrating on one lure, learning everything it could do in the water, then moving to another.

Looking back, it was amazing to have the luxury of an entire year to practice each lure. Nobody has that kind of time . . . except a kid! Adults can't pull it off. We're too busy earning a living. At the 2000 Bassmaster Classic, the West Coast anglers kicked everyone's butts drop shotting— tying on their bait, then running another ten inches of line down to a weight on the bottom. I wanted to learn the technique, but was lucky to find two or three days afterward to play around with it. Twelve months? Forget about it!

Taking Advantage of the Revolution

I was lucky to grow up during an explosion of information about fishing. With magazines, television, and videos, I was able to learn faster than guys who came up only ten or fifteen years before me. Media has had an enormous impact on the popularity and growth of the sport. Here's a breakdown of some important developments.

THE BASSMASTERS TELEVISION SHOW

Bob Cobb created *The Bassmasters* television series, which debuted in 1985. He was basically the entire operation, serving as producer, editor, director, intern, and secretary. It was the first time competitive bass fishing hit the airwaves, which was huge in shaping the careers of younger anglers. Catching my first bass in the Poconos and reading *Bassmaster* magazine charged my interest, but the moment I tuned in to *The Bassmasters,* everything reached a whole new level. For me, Saturday morning wasn't about cartoons, music videos, or watching baseball. It was about tuning to The Nashville Network, waiting for *The Bassmasters* to start. Early on, the coverage wasn't advanced, but it still was amazing. As a teenager, I can vividly remember getting chills watching Rick Clunn and Ken Cook winning Classics. It was absolutely riveting, and made me want to do what they did.

Early episodes made stars out of a lot of guys, and helped put a face on the sport. They created an explosion of other fishing programs, as guys like Roland Martin and Bill Dance parlayed huge charisma into getting their own shows. Even as a kid, I was very conscious of which anglers showed emotion and personality on the water. I looked at a guy like Denny Brauer, thinking, "Wow! He's cool!" On the flip side, I remember watching Ray Scott try to prompt some energy out of Bo Dowden, Jr., while he was weighing in nearly thirty pounds at some event on Lake Seminole. All Bo mustered was a deadpan "Well . . . the good Lord blessed me today. See if we can do it tomorrow." Cue crickets and tumbleweeds. Bo's probably a super guy and he's definitely a great angler. But to teenagers watching, charismatic guys like Larry Nixon shined brightest. It's also because of *The Bassmasters* that anglers grew more professional and well-spoken, because big sponsorships always go to the most presentable personalities. As with all major sports, television completely revolutionized the bass-fishing landscape.

THE VHS REVOLUTION

As fishing on TV started blowing up, so did series upon series of fishing videos people could watch at home. One of the most famous, which I must have watched a thousand times, was called *Bigmouth*, and was made by Glen Lau. It shows underwater footage, following the life cycle of bass from spawn to birth, maturing to feeding. There's not a word about technique. But everything about it seemed bigger than life. Then there were the Bass Pro Shops videos, which highlighted the styles and techniques of different anglers. They were like the skateboarding videos that became really popular in the eighties, exposing people to a sport that wasn't very popular at the time, and blowing their minds. For the first time, the Tony Hawk generation could keep rewinding that Ollie until they mastered it. It was the same for me with an instructional video on how to fish topwater from Bass Pro Shops. I was constantly rewinding, watching, imitating, and learning.

4
IKE THE COLLECTOR

Even as a baby, I was constantly in motion, which didn't change as I got older. I was always hustling around, from breakdancing to hockey to fishing, with other sports like baseball tossed in for kicks. I was one busy little dude. And like most little dudes, I wanted to be cool. I didn't think fishing qualified, so I kept it pretty quiet, sharing it only with good friends. But I had another hobby—collecting—which made fishing seem as cool as being in a biker gang. All fishermen have a collector gene, since a huge part of fishing's appeal comes from building a collection of lures, even ones that never actually hit the water. They're just fun to look at and talk about. But my collecting jones started, ridiculously (and slightly embarrassingly) enough, with butterflies. I'm not kidding. For as long as I can remember, my mom has loved butterflies. During those early Poconos trips, we'd go into the woods, trying to collect as many species as possible. Then we'd get them home, euthanize the poor little guys, and mount them in display cases. Tough luck for the butterflies, but Mom loved it, and I loved making her happy. But even as a seven-year-old, I knew not to run around school bragging about my butterfly fetish. Except to Bobby Soaker, another kindergartener weird enough to collect butterflies.

Around the fourth grade, I swapped butterflies for treasure hunting with my uncle. He bought me a kiddie metal detector and we'd head out into fields and parks, looking for old coins and stuff. It seemed silly at the beginning, but once we started pulling silver quarters and dimes from the eighteen hundreds—worth a couple hundred bucks a pop—I got pretty into it. The killer stuff was over in Fairmont Park in north-west Philly. We were lucky not to encounter *actual* killers, since Fairmont Park dips into some of Philly's worst neighborhoods. But Don's a big dude, and he was in pretty good shape in those days, so I guess we were safe.

We eventually read something about bottle collecting, which is actually a hard-core subculture of the treasure-hunting world, and decided to give that a try. We'd do some research and find old town dumps from the eighteenth and nineteenth centuries, then dig them up, looking for old bottles. Sometimes we'd dig through privies, where people once dug holes for outhouses (two hundred years later, everything is decomposed, so it's not as bad as it sounds). I was finding old medicine and cologne bottles sometimes worth thirty dollars each. When you're twelve, that's like winning the lottery. As I got older, I obsessively collected old ink bottles, the kind used for quill pens, then later for fountain pens. I even hit weekend swap meets to trade with collectors from all over the country. I knew my stuff, too! I could tell an ink bottle's age and carried a black light to find flaws and repairs. I built up an impressive collection, which I still have today, stored at my uncle's place. He'd better take care of it, too, since it's probably worth more than fifteen thousand dollars.

Iaconelli: Rhymes with Gretzky (Sort of)

Growing up, the other major part of my life, equally as important as fishing, was hockey. I got hooked on street hockey around age six, running around trying to keep the ball out of the gutter, moving the nets when cars came. "Game on! Game off!" just like in *Wayne's World.* As I got older, I moved to deck hockey, which was played in a rink on a really awesome plastic surface that made the game incredibly fast. Everything was identical to ice hockey, except the ice and the price. You needed more gear for ice hockey, and the ice time was incredibly expensive. On the flip side, I could play deck hockey for around $150 a season, which included big Northeast tournaments with serious cash prizes. I'm talking in the thousands, you know? And because deck hockey was so widespread and affordable, I kept playing into my twenties, until fishing and deejaying, a hobby I'd pick up later that would eventually become a minicareer, took up too much of my time.

One of the best teams I ever organized was the Ball Hogs, sponsored by J&L Poultry, a Camden, NJ–based meat wholesaler that sold poultry and hogs. Our logo was a pig holding a stick (clever, huh?). One of my greatest athletic moments—and all-time freak-outs—came in a tournament I played with the Ball Hogs. In one of those perfect, dramatic moments, I ripped a wrist shot top shelf over the goalie's blocker in overtime, which won us the gold. Anybody who played with me in that league wasn't surprised to see me "go Ike" after catching the winning fish in the '03 Classic, because after I scored, I leaped up onto the boards and screamed "YEAAAAAHHHH!" holding on to the fence that separated me from the *other team's* fans. I was possessed, man! Then I jumped off the boards and got mobbed by my teammates. It couldn't get any better that that!

Like everything else in my life, I gave hockey 110 percent. Similar to when I was mastering new lures, I used to practice for hours, trying to perfect specific shots and moves. Because I was so small, I had to outwork my opponents or I'd get killed. I used to look up to guys like Wayne Gretzky and Mario Lemieux, but my favorite player was Bobby Clarke of the Philadelphia Flyers. He wasn't the biggest, strongest, or most skilled guy on the ice, but he made himself into one of the NHL's most feared players because he had more heart than anyone. That's how I saw myself when I played hockey, and it's how I see myself in fishing. I'm no natural like Larry Nixon, who you could drop blindfolded onto any body of water in the world and he'd still catch fish. I have to push myself from the moment I start doing research to the moment I pull into the landing on the last day of the tournament. That's how I keep my edge over guys who are more talented than me.

THE UNIQUE ROCKERS

Up until seventh grade, I was into rock and metal bands, dudes like Ozzy Osbourne, Rush, and that classic New Jersey staple, Journey. Then break-dancing blew up in South Jersey and hit me like a ton of bricks. The movement, the action, and especially the music. Breakdancing is closely tied to the beginnings of hip-hop, a style of music that spoke to me the moment I heard it. Listening to pioneers like Kurtis Blow, Big Daddy Kane, Red Alert, and especially Run-D.M.C., just blew me away. Even today, after all these years, I'm still amazed when I listen to their stuff.

During the seventh grade, I formed my first breakin' crew, called the Unique Rockers, about seven or eight guys from Runnemede. Dudes like Brian Wilkenson, Sonny Sonessa, Vinnie Denesse, his brother Mike, and Ronny Pasquarello (with those names, you'd think we were auditioning for *The Sopranos*). We were totally hard core, practicing obsessively anytime and anyplace we could, including the back room of my uncle's house. It wasn't just fishing where I was a preparation and practice junkie! Initially we put cardboard on the floor to keep friction from slowing down our spinning moves, but eventually we replaced it with a huge piece of linoleum. You know you've made it when you've upgraded to linoleum, baby!

BREAKIN' BATTLES   Early competition just meant kicking everyone's butt in talent shows around town and in school. But the Unique Rockers wanted to test our boundaries, so we set up "battles" where we'd square off against crews from neighboring towns like Bellmawr and Glendora. I was competitive even then, and we took our dance-offs very seriously. We'd get ourselves all duded out in matching black and red Puma tracksuits (our official colors), Kangol hats, Jordache jeans, and Adidas with as many different colored superwide laces as we could stuff in the eyes. You'd also have your breakin' name sewn on the jacket. Mine was simply "Ike." It's always been my nickname. We'd either walk to the neighboring town, which was a hassle, or have our moms drive us, which was less of a hassle but more embarrassing. Then we'd square off in fire halls, gymnasiums, the skating rink, at teen dances, or in any other space we could find. We even took trips to Philly and New York. The whole thing had a very *West Side Story* feel to it, except without the singing.

Battles worked like this. You'd request whatever song you wanted from the DJ. (I was partial to "Captain Rock to the Future Shock" by Captain Rock, and "Planet Rock" by Afrika Bambaataa & the Soul Sonic Force.) Then you'd move to the center of the floor and put your skills head-to-head against guys from other crews. We'd take turns busting moves, like guitar players trading fours. The first of my showstoppers was Suicide Windmills, where you spin around on your shoulders, legs spread like windmill blades. But my signature move was the 1990, where I'd spin on one hand like a top. In my prime, I could hit seven rotations, which was pretty sick! (Not impressed? Go ahead and try . . . but call your orthopedist first.) After we finished, it was basically up to the audience to decide who won. And sometimes you'd win more than just their applause. One night in eighth grade, after a battle at Bellmawr Fire Hall, I met the first girl that I really liked, Colleen Malone. We even ended up dating for a while. I don't know if it was kosher to go into the next town and steal one of their women, but who cares! She was hot!

As ridiculous as some of this was, looking back on it, breakin' and fishing had a lot of parallels. Take competition. When we'd battle another crew, it was heated. But afterward, we had respect for the skills everyone flashed, and made friends (one of my best friends, Bill Graves, is a guy I met when he was in a rival crew). Same thing happens on the water. I don't give an inch to Kevin VanDam, Denny Brauer, or anyone else, but once the boats are hitched up, I love spending time with them, shooting the breeze. Another similarity? My obsession to perfect everything I do. Early on in my breakin' career, I had trouble with head spins, where you kick up and spin around on the top of your head. I nearly wore a hole in my skull trying to perfect it. Kind of like the hours I spent as a teenager trying to master every lure under the sun. Breakin' and fishing. Different sports. Same mentality.

5 FISHING IN THE CLOSET

Young Bruce Wayne

By the time I hit high school, I was getting out on the water at least a couple of times a week with a few close fishing buddies. On off days, I flipped lures at pots and soda bottles in the backyard and devoured the newest issue of *Bassmaster*. But I still felt like there'd be a social stigma attached to fishing, so I wasn't open about it in public. I was known for playing hockey, and then for being a DJ. I started spinning during my freshman year, and to be honest, I kinda sucked. My beats were way, way off, and I had a lot to learn. But as with anything I've ever wanted in life, I practiced my butt off, and by my senior year I worked the "wheels of steel" pretty good. I was booking gigs at high schools and parties. Everywhere. I was making legitimate money, and for a long time I thought that might be how I'd make a living.

Hockey and spinning were great for maintaining a social life, and like any kid, I wanted to be cool. I didn't think South Jersey was a place where fishing would impress people, especially girls. "Hey, baby, you want to see me cast my grub?" Not exactly the greatest pick-up line.

Until my senior year, it was like I had a split personality. In the Poconos I could be the hard-core fisherman, because nobody was there but my family. Pulling bass after bass out of the water made me a rock star in their eyes. Unfortunately, what's cool to your family may not be so cool in the halls of Triton High. So I was the fishing equivalent of Batman, with a secret angler identity. Whenever I could sneak away, I was the Caped Crusader, hitting any fishery I could find around Runnemede. But to all but a select few, I was still just Bruce Wayne (without the mansion and butler, of course).

COMING OUT OF THE CLOSET

We used to have great parties out on Axel's Lake, a thin, L-shaped sand quarry lake with super good swimming. It was so isolated, we could light a wicked bonfire without getting hassled. We'd bring cases and cases of beer, party all night, then throw down blankets and crash out on the beach. But Axel's wasn't just great for partying. Its deep, clear water also made it a tremendous fishery. That presented a problem for my yin and yang personality. On the one hand, I wanted to be cool. On the other hand, I didn't want to miss a crack at a killer lake.

In the end, killer lake won.

Besides, all the hiding and sneaking around was getting ridiculous. I liked to fish. Who cared? So while these huge lake parties were going down, I'd grab a beer and head off with my rod and reel. But here's the funny part. After almost ten years of hiding, after building up in my head that I'd be committing social suicide the minute I made my first cast in public, you know what reaction I got? None. Nobody cared. Actually, I take that back. A couple of people actually thought it was pretty cool. I was still "Mike the DJ" and "Mike the Hockey Player," but now I was also "Mike the Fisherman" and didn't care who knew. Batman had retired his utility belt.

MIKE'S ULTIMATE DJ MIX

Whether you're spinning vinyl for a crowd of two hundred or setting up your iPod for some road trip music, your collection of tunes won't be complete without the following.

1. *Afrika Bambaataa & the Soul Sonic Force*
SONG OR ALBUM "Planet Rock"
COMMENT The best breaking song ever!

2. *Run-D.M.C.*
SONG OR ALBUM "Peter Piper"
COMMENT My favorite song to cut and scratch. I can go back and forth on the records for hours!

3. *Eric B & Rakim*
SONG OR ALBUM "Paid in Full"
COMMENT The hottest hip-hop beat and rhymes ever made.

4. *Tuff Crew*
SONG OR ALBUM "My Part of Town"
COMMENT You can't help but dance to this classic song. Plus they're from my area. Got to support the local scene.

5. *Deftones*
SONG OR ALBUM *Adrenaline*
COMMENT Put this in when you're mad at the world. This is my favorite album of all time!

6. *Korn*
SONG OR ALBUM "Shoots and Ladders"
COMMENT My favorite mosh pit song. I had my fair share of stitches after moshing to this one.

7. *Taproot*

SONG OR ALBUM *Gift*

COMMENT A great album with a lot of deep meaning. This album helped me through a lot of tough times.

8. *Slipknot*

SONG OR ALBUM "Wait and Bleed"

COMMENT Great motivational music for the gym. Put on this song to get rid of your stress.

9. *The Notorious B.I.G.*

SONG OR ALBUM *Ready To Die*

COMMENT The best rapper of his time. Amazing lyrical flow.

10. *Nas*

SONG OR ALBUM *Illmatic*

COMMENT This album helped bring rap back to the forefront. In college, the song "Halftime" was played nonstop.

11. *50 Cent*

SONG OR ALBUM *Get Rich or Die Trying*

COMMENT I played this nonstop when I won the Classic. A lot of good times were spent listening to this album.

12. *Jay-Z*

SONG OR ALBUM *The Black Album*

COMMENT Jay-Z's farewell, and a farewell to all the negatives of 2003!

Show and Tell

If I didn't put the final nail in my "secret angler" coffin at Axel's, I did it during a public speaking class I took that year in school. Mrs. Schumacher, a totally hot teacher everyone had a thing for, gave an assignment where we had to stand in front of the class and give a step-by-step demonstration of something. At the time, I had trouble talking about anything in front of people (surprising, but true) unless I knew a lot about it. So the weekend before my presentation I caught a crappie at Axel's, then brought it to school and filleted it for the class. I marched to the front of the room, whipped out this huge-bladed fillet knife (can you imagine bringing one to school today?), and started slicing. Guts and blood splattered everywhere. Some people, especially some of the girls, were completely grossed out. But everyone was intrigued as I cut that little panfish into beautiful fillets. Ms. Schumacher must be an outdoorsman at heart, because I received one of my best grades of the year on that project. From there on, reentering the fishing closet wasn't an option. Once you start slicing up your hobby in front of the class, it's not really a secret anymore.

Meeting Kristi

But it wasn't just coming out of the fishing closet that made senior year memorable. That's also when I met Kristi. I was out with Tom Hrynyshyn in my Toyota pickup, cruising the neighborhood, which had a specific route and was a whole production. It started in the mall parking lot. We'd take a lap around the mall, then head across the street to make a pass in front of the movie theater. We'd finish, of course, with a lap around McDonald's, then we'd park for a while and eventually start again. It was so stupid, but everyone else was doing the same thing, so we were just part of the circuit. And Kristi was out and about, hanging with her friend Colleen (not the girl from the Bellmawr Fire Hall battle). Honestly, I was more into her friend at the beginning. We pulled over and started a conversation with them, because I wanted to talk to Colleen. They gave us a phone number and said to call, but it was Kristi's, not Colleen's. A couple of weeks later, I was drinking with my buddy John Carter—a dude who was so skinny and bony we called him Skeletor—and said, "Let's call this number and see what they're doing." So I called, and instead of just talking like normal people, we totally messed with them instead, never saying who we were. The next time I saw Kristi she busted me, and I admitted to it. For whatever reason, she was actually willing to keep talking to me afterward. The most significant relationship I've ever had was off and running.

6 TOP ROD BASSMASTERS

Even in elementary school, I was an organizer. From the Unique Rockers to the deck hockey teams I started, I liked putting groups together. But my best accomplishment of all would be Top Rod Bassmasters, the fishing club I helped establish. It's still in existence today, over thirty members strong. But Top Rod's beginnings were considerably more humble.

Putting It Together

By the time I graduated high school, I was way out of the fishing closet and didn't care who thought I was a weirdo. In fact, I was concerned about finding more competitive outlets than just the half dozen or so local buddy tournaments available to me each year. In the summer of '91 I started calling the local "big boat clubs," whose members drove big Ranger bass boats, as opposed to the little johnboat I still trolled around in. None was interested in having a rider join. I was upset, because I knew I could outfish any of them! So I had two choices: look under the mattress to check to see if I had hidden $40,000 for a boat, or start my own club.

I was just out of high school, and knew what was under my mattress. So I gathered together four of my friends who love to fish and we started our own club. John McGraw, Brian Stockl, Dave Brodzek, Chris Dalfonso, and I were the hard-core five, the original members of Top Rod Bassmasters. Dalfonso and Stockl were total naturals, as good as anyone I've ever seen. McGraw and Brodzek were no slackers either. We wrote to BASS, and they sent us a packet explaining what we needed to do to become a sanctioned, affiliated club. Right away, we had a problem. According to the guidelines, you needed six guys to start an affiliated club. So we roped in a high school buddy, Steve Pellegrino, who occasionally fished with us, but was barely a soft-core angler, much less hard-core. But he was a good sport, put in for dues, and became the official sixth member. He never made a meeting or fished a club tournament, but that first year Steve was as important to the club as anybody. Without him, we were literally nonexistent!

We set up a pair of single-day tournaments each month. The first was invitational style, fishing head-to-head in our johnboats. The second was a buddy format, where we competed in pairs. Since we had only five dudes that first year, the sixth spot in the buddy tournaments was taken by anybody we could scrape up. My uncle Don fished a couple, Dave's cousin joined in for a few others. Then, on the first Tuesday of every month, we'd get together—with a case of beer—for our club meeting. We'd get the stupid business stuff out of the way ASAP, then talk fishing. The club's philosophy could be summarized with one word: learning. We drove each other to learn and improve, intentionally scheduling club tournaments on as many different lakes and environments as we could find. We hit ponds, reservoirs, and tidal water, areas with muddy, clear, or cedar water (also called Pinelands water, it's full of decaying plant life). At the next meeting, we'd share information about the last tournament, so we could all learn what worked, what didn't, and why. We were all at that stage of development where there was no such thing as too much information. Every insight and experience helped make us better. It was an amazing approach, and one that I totally recommend for other clubs, especially those with young anglers.

The truly sick thing was, even though we had only five or six guys in these tournaments, I was so competitive I'd practice for days. How ridiculous is that? All we had on the line was pride and a little pocket money. I guarantee I spent way more than the sixty-dollar winner's "purse" replacing equipment that broke during practice. You could make an argument that I was a tad too competitive. I'm sure the rest of the Top Rod guys would agree. (Eventually, the club voted not to have prize money in the invitational style tournaments. I guess everyone got tired of me taking their cash every month!)

My Real *First Classic Win*

The bylaws our first year stated that our top five point-getters made the Club Classic. Well, there were only five guys in the freakin' club, so congratulations! Finally, a tournament it was impossible *not* to qualify for. To choose the location, each member wrote the name of a fishery on a piece of paper and tossed it in a hat, then we pulled one name. That first year, and for the next two, Alloway Lake was pulled. This was an amazing little private lake, which, like many lakes in Jersey, was created when the local stream was dammed in the eighteen hundreds. It didn't take long for it to become one of my all-time favorites.

Even though there were only five guys competing and the results didn't mean anything, the first Top Rod Club Classic still felt sort of historic. It was the finale to something we all had a hand in creating. So everyone was dead set on winning, but from the moment I stepped into my johnboat, I just crushed 'em. It was the first tournament in which I got into what athletes call "the zone," where nothing existed except me and the fish. Every move becomes the right move. Every cast becomes the right cast. Interestingly, one of the lures I was skipping under the docks and brush was a black and blue Stone Jig. It was one of the original models, which McGraw and I had invented and later poured in my grandmom's house. Twelve years later, I threw that lure (in a more evolved form) on the Louisiana Delta in the Bassmaster Classic. So really, when I hoisted that Classic trophy over my head in New Orleans in '03, I was just reenacting my real first Classic win.

LESSONS LEARNED

The strategies and techniques I learned during my Top Rod days are the same ones I now use on the BASS and FLW (Forrest L. Wood) Tours. I'm not just talking about straight techniques like proficiency and accuracy. I learned about casting positions. Boat angles. Negotiating traffic on the water. Time management. Decision making under pressure. Even culling, the process of picking which fish to let go when you've got your five-fish limit, so you can catch another. But the biggest leaps came in my mental game. In Top Rod, I learned to behave like a tournament angler. I had to stay focused and consistent whether I was killing them, like I did during that first Club Classic, or I was struggling, like I was during our second Club Classic, where I really had to grind it out. With about twenty minutes left, my bag was too small and I was basically out of ideas. Then I noticed that over the course of the day, a pile of leaves had gathered up by a tree near the launch. It was a subtle change in the environment, but change can be key. I gave it one more shot, pulled out a five-pounder, and won. I was proud of myself for never quitting, and for staying observant of the environment from start to finish. That's how tournament anglers fish.

So when our third Classic rolled around the following fall, I thought I was money, especially since, for the third year running, it would be

JIGS

Mention jigs, and many people picture an old school, rubber-skirted half-ounce bait with a pork trailer, used solely for bottom-fishing sluggish bass in cooler water. Those people are missing out. Jigs are quite possibly the most versatile bait out there and work year-round. They come in more colors than an acid trip, match any environment, and can employ an endless variety of trailers. If I had to put one lure in my box to use all year, it'd be a jig. There are as many jig color combinations as there are colors, but three of my favorites include a black-blue, which imitates a molting crawfish, green pumpkin with orange (resembling bluegill and sunfish), and white-blue (like shad). Ninety percent of the time I'll be throwing a Stone Jig, but I'll occasionally use a hair jig (bear, duck feathers, and caribou are my favorites).

While jigs can be used year-round, it's important to adjust your strategy depending on the season.

WINTER. When the water temperature drops, I'll fish a jig in a traditional style—on the bottom, slow and low. Winter is probably the only time I actually attach a stereotypical pork trailer, maybe an 11A or No. 1 pork, imitating those crawfish wintering at the bottom of a fishery.

SPRING. In the pre-spawn period, the bass start becoming more active, and so do the crawfish. I'll stick with a jig resembling a crawfish, but I'll hop it a little more, and might even add a single-tailed plastic grub. The increased action resembles a crawfish emerging from hibernation. This strategy can really pack your live well once you master it.

Right around the end of spring, in the post-spawn period, fish start to suspend, especially in a fishery heavy with treetops and logs like Santee Cooper in South Carolina, or places like Lake Murray or Guntersville, which are loaded with vegetation. The fish are recovering from the hard work of spawning (hey, we all need a little rest after that), and are looking to recuperate with an easy meal. I'll capitalize on that by swimming a jig past their faces, almost like a spinnerbait waving through the water column, which prompts a quality reaction strike. I particularly like this technique when the bass are suspended on docks and other solid cover.

SUMMER. Want a great summertime reaction-strike strategy? Scout the fishery for steep vertical or channel banks, then take a larger jig, anywhere from one-half to one ounce, and crash it down the stair step or the vertical break, bouncing that jig down to the lower depths of the water column. This delivers the jig perfectly to those heat-shunning bass in the deep water and encourages a quality strike. The crashing strategy will work great for you all season.

FALL. Time to think outside the box a little, and do what I call "popping a jig." I'll take a jig in a shad color, like white or Mike's Special Color (a light blue, gray, and light brown lure I helped create with Mann's designed to imitate clear-water crawfish), and actually pop it like a spoon. The jig bounces vertically off the bottom through the schooling baitfish such as shad, and when the bass are making easy meals out of those schools, it works great. The popping action is the key during fall fishing.

held on Alloway. I owned that fishery. It was mine! Unfortunately, nobody told the fish that I was supposed to win. I couldn't figure them out or even catch a limit. But I was still confident, since I was Señor Top Rod. If I finished with a weak little bag, so would everyone else, right? Not this time. Dave just crushed 'em, arriving at the dock with a fat bag and a huge grin. Meanwhile, I didn't even finish second! I was so angry, and analyzed every little thing I screwed up and what I should have done instead. But in the end, the biggest mistake I made was assuming before the day had started that nobody could beat me. I always believe I can win if I fish to my ability. But you should never *assume* victory. Major lesson learned. You haven't won anything until you're handed a trophy and a check.

In the end, I was proud of Dave for stepping up his game. We created the club so everyone would become a better fisherman, and it was working. What's cool, too, is that if you look at Top Rod Bassmasters now, it really hasn't changed. It's still a small boat club for guys who want to improve and share knowledge, the perfect place to spend three or four years advancing your skills for the next level. The original guys eventually outgrew the club and stepped up to bigger boats, and were replaced by the next generation. Even though I'm only an honorary member now, I still feel a lot of pride about Top Rod, like watching one of your kids grow up.

7 GROWING UP

Graduating from High School

When I graduated from Triton High School, most people still thought of me primarily as a hockey-playing disc jockey. People knew I fished, but it's not like I walked around in fishing hats with baits hooked on. I was pretty social, moving back and forth between the different cliques at school. I had friends all over the place, although by the time graduation rolled around, there was *one* group where I definitely didn't fit in: guys going to college. I didn't even bother applying. Looking back, it's not surprising. I had done just enough to get by, a C student with mediocre SATs. I felt like once I graduated, that was it for school. Needless to say, my family was disappointed, especially my uncle. He had gone to Temple University in Philadelphia, but dropped out right before he graduated, a decision he always told me he regretted. While they couldn't force me to go to school, if I was going to live at home they demanded I get a job. I was still making some money as a DJ, but it wasn't steady enough. I had to get a "real job." Once I entered the working world, college looked pretty good, pretty fast.

The Job That Sold Me on College

My buddy Brian and I got jobs at Accumark, a humongous shipping and receiving company that contracts with all sorts of companies, including Macy's, making twelve dollars an hour. It seemed like really good money at the time . . . until we realized our job was lugging and loading boxes onto conveyor belts so they could get shipped out. If hauling endless boxes in an incredibly hot New Jersey warehouse sounds fun to you, by all means, sign up. It was crazy how many screwed-up people I met on the job. Ultimately, though, they provided more than just sick entertainment. One really bizarre dude, who we called "Edgar A. Hairbomb" because his hair was all over the place, would always say, "Yeah, I got this job right out of high school, fifteen years ago. . . . But this is just temporary." Serious reality check! And plenty of incentive to get back to school ASAP. I didn't last even a year at Accumark.

Juco to Rowan

When I told my family I was going back to school, they were totally stoked. Unfortunately, my high school transcripts were so crappy I couldn't get into a halfway decent school, so I enrolled in Camden County Community College. I had no idea what direction I wanted to go in academically, but since writing was one of the only things I enjoyed in high school, I steered toward marketing classes, film classes, and other courses that required tons of it. After working my butt off for two years, I narrowed my focus to advertising and public relations. I was eventually admitted to Rowan University and East Stroudsburg University, but chose Rowan because I could commute, staying closer to my family and

Kristi. In the fall of '93, the guy who didn't even bother sending off an application out of high school officially became a full-fledged college student. My outlook had totally changed. Getting good grades and a bachelor's degree was now a high priority. I even used the same preparation and study methods in school as I did researching fisheries. My skills were pretty advanced. Fishing was actually paying off academically, something I would never have imagined.

But just as in high school, I was still juggling a million things at once. The fishing club, deejaying, school, maintaining my relationship with Kristi. Weekends were constant motion. I had turned my freelance DJ gig into a real, full-fledged business, and was spinning music on Fridays until 2:00 A.M., getting home, packing up the boat, then sleeping two or three hours before Saturday's Top Rod tournament. I'd grab another hour of sleep once I got off the water, and be back at a club spinning that night, all while trying to squeeze in some time together with Kristi. My responsibilities with school, deejaying, and my personal life were growing at the same rate as my Top Rod career, and everything was starting to collide. But instead of scaling back my fishing, I decided to take it up a notch. I had been in the club for three years and growing pains were setting in. I wanted to expand my horizons and take the next step up the ladder. So I filled out the paperwork and entered the pro-am tournaments on the amateur side. So much for extra sleep.

8
IKE THE AMATEUR

Lake Norman, vol. I (1992)

All I needed to get into my first pro-am on the BASS circuit in the fall of '92 was a checkbook and luck. You pick the tournaments you want to fish, send a deposit, and BASS randomly draws who gets in, and for which tournament. Either you're lucky enough to get picked or you're not. I was lucky, and drew the North Carolina Top 100, held on Lake Norman in North Carolina, part of the '92–'93 BASS season. I was absolutely psyched to fish the biggest event of my life.

What a Rook

All I'd fished up to this point were local money and club tournaments out of my johnboat. From the moment I walked into registration, I was totally blown away! I was seeing anglers that I'd read about for almost ten years, my heroes of the sport. I didn't say a word to anybody, though. It was like a high school dance, where the cool kids hang out and socialize, and the dorks sit in the corner and watch. We amateurs were the dorks, sitting there slack-jawed, going, "Whoa! That's Larry Nixon! There's Rick Clunn!" Then they called my name. "Runnemede, New Jersey. Waggoner, Oklahoma. Mike Iaconelli, Tommy Biffle." Tommy Biffle? Awesome! My first day, and I drew a giant in the sport. I was nervous meeting him, but he turned out to be the mellowest dude in the world. "Yeah, we're gonna fish some topwater in the morning, then hit some docks. It's tough out here, but the water's clear . . ." and so on and so on. Totally cool. Tommy was staying at the Days Inn and suggested we meet there at 5 A.M. It was perfect, because I was at the Best Western, right across the street. I got his room number, and everything was set. Super easy.

The next morning, I was ready with time to spare. I walked over to the Days Inn and knocked on Biffle's door. 5:00 A.M., right on time. No answer. Knock again. Still no answer. I walked down to the front desk and asked, "What room's Tommy Biffle in?" The woman checked, and wrinkled her face. "We don't have a Tommy Biffle here, but there's another Days Inn in Mooresville." Uh-oh. He was in the next town over. I didn't even know there was a Mooresville!

Aaaaaaggggggghhh!

It's the first day of the biggest tournament of my life, and I'd already screwed up. I didn't know what to do, so I just scrambled to the ramp and met Biffle at the launch. Picture this total amateur running down the dock with his tackle box and rods. It was so bad. And I could see Biffle in his boat, rolling his eyes, thinking, "Jesus, I've got this idiot all day?" He was frazzled too, because waiting for me threw him off his schedule. Fortunately, I didn't have much time to worry, because soon our number was called. All of a sudden . . . blastoff! Tommy cranked his boat up to 75 mph, peeling my face back and nearly making me wet

REGIONAL DIFFERENCES

Lake Norman was the first big tournament I'd ever fished outside my Northeast home base. I knew I'd have to make adjustments in North Carolina, because of regional differences between fisheries across the country. The U.S. can basically be divided into three large regions. The Northeast, the South, and the West. (These divisions are a little fuzzy, of course, because the U.S. is so big, but in general terms, they hold true.) Each region's unique qualities call for certain skills, which explains why guys from particular regions specialize in certain techniques. But to be a truly great fisherman, you need to be able to fish in any environment, using the techniques critical to each region. Here's how it breaks down.

THE SOUTH. I look at this area as a huge box, the four points being Virginia, Florida, Texas, and Ohio. (Yeah, I'm aware which side of the Mason-Dixon Line Ohio is on, but we're talking fishing geography here, not actual geography.) When I think of southern fisheries, their major advantage is climate. The weather stays warm longer, meaning a longer growing season and larger bass. Up in the Northeast, a five-pound fish is huge, but in Alabama it's nothing spectacular. You won't impress people until you start pulling out eight-pounders. Second, the warmer weather means a longer fishing season. A fisherman in Florida can fish year-round, whereas Jersey guys might be iced out for four months of the year. That's a major advantage in a Southerner's skill development.

The South is great for my style of power fishing, throwing big baits at cover using heavy line, and working large stretches of water. When you think of the South, you imagine guys flipping docks and trees, or aggressive crankbait fishing along a stretch of riprap. Large bodies of water, and lots of man-made reservoirs, with stained or muddy water and tons of cover: docks, trees, brush piles, wood, and lay downs (trees that have fallen into the water from the bank). Down south, people use crankbaits and spinnerbaits to cover huge stretches of water, and they land big fish.

THE WEST. This area includes everything west of the Mississippi, including Colorado, New Mexico, California, and Utah. The polar opposite of the South, western fisheries feature deep, crystal-clear water, vertical canyon walls, and lots of rock on the bottom, without much wood, brush, lay downs, or other forms of cover. While the South has plenty of lakes, allowing anglers to spread out, the West has only a few high-quality fisheries. That means the good ones, including Lake Mead, Lake Havasu, Lake Powell, and Clear Lake, get tons of boat pressure. The fish see a lot of lures, and by fish standards get pretty smart. A good limit out west might be ten pounds. The tough conditions lend themselves to finesse fishing—using light line, like a clear or fluorocarbon, on spinning equipment, on small, three- to four-inch baits. The deep water also forces anglers to get creative. Guys like Skeet Reese and Aaron Martins have mastered tactics like drop shotting, where a hook is attached directly to the line, twelve to eighteen inches above a sinker, and spoon jigging, where a jig is bounced off the bottom like a spoon. They're also great at using electronics to read the fishery, since you can almost never see the bottom.

THE NORTH. Technically, it's really the Northeast. Jersey, Pennsylvania, all the states along the Atlantic north of

Maryland, and Michigan. Our major disadvantage is weather. Some kid in Georgia had way more time on the water to perfect techniques than I did growing up. I had to compensate by poring over magazines and videos and casting at backyard targets in the snow. At least now, with the Internet, it's easier to gain knowledge in the off-season, helping anglers start off more prepared when spring comes.

The North combines many features of the South and West, but on a smaller scale. Like Southern lakes, ours have lots of cover. We've got the trees, the docks, and lay downs. One aspect we excel at is weed fishing, since that kind of natural vegetation is all over the region. Our water is also often clear and deep like out west, and we unfortunately share their boat pressure problems, too. A big body of water in New Jersey is three thousand acres, barely a cove on a southern or western fishery. So despite having many good lakes, outside of monsters like the Great Lakes or Lake Champlain, there isn't much room to spread out. So our fish, like the ones out West, can be pretty picky. To be successful in the North, you'll need Southern power tactics, but also Western finesse styles. It's a sort of catch-22. Northern anglers are exposed to a wider variety of conditions than Southern and Western guys, but we have a smaller window of time each year to hone our skills on the water.

In the end, a fisherman from anywhere in the country can excel if he's willing to learn and adapt. It just takes a lot of time, energy, and above all, hard work . . . the kind I've put in my entire career.

myself. This was fast! The biggest boats I'd ever ridden at that point were powered by little 9-9 kickers or 15's. Nothing like the giant 150-horsepower engines the pros use. My butt flew off the seat as we hit the waves! I was stoked and terrified all at once. But I was in a real tournament, and loving every second.

You Don't Know Jack, Iaconelli

I was completely in awe that first day, but I still paid close attention to everything Tommy did. I noticed how he trimmed the length of his jig skirts and sharpened his hooks up instead of down. He used superglue to attach trailers to his jig, which was fascinating to watch. Biffle is a power fisherman, and I watched as he flipped docks, putting his jig in places that I couldn't imagine at the time. I was just starting to figure out conventional rods, but still using spinning equipment the majority of the time. I was just in awe of Biffle's mechanics and accuracy. I had two Top Rod Classic wins under my belt and was our angler of the year. I thought I was the man. I was wrong.

The other lesson I learned was that when the competition was on, it was *on*. We had reached a topwater area by some riprap, which is where Biffle wanted to start. There was a boat off in the distance, and all of a sudden . . . vrrrrrooooom! It was hauling toward us, with Denny Brauer behind the wheel! And he just unloaded on Tommy. "You knew I was fishing this stretch in the morning! You saw me here in practice!" I didn't know what the hell to think. On the one hand, it's Denny Brauer, one of the legends! But he was also furious, and in person he is a big, imposing dude. I was this weird combination of starstruck and scared to death. Should I ask for an autograph, or cry? The day was already memorable and I hadn't even thrown a cast yet.

Tommy eventually pulled up his trolling motor and gave Denny the spot. But not without some grumbling later on. "I don't know what he's so upset about. That's not Denny's stretch." And he was probably right. Fishing is governed by an unwritten code that says if two people are fighting over a particular spot, it goes to the guy who had established himself there first, or the guy who is higher in the standings. It was the first day of the tournament. Nobody had established themselves there in competition (practice doesn't count), and there were no standings yet. But Tommy left, and that made it Denny's spot for sure. I'm sure Denny was genuinely upset, but he was mostly trying to intimidate Tommy into leaving a space he wanted. I've seen Tommy and Denny off the water, laughing and having a good time. It wasn't anything personal, it was just competition. Everyone is out there to win.

That first day was one I'll never forget. I had my first taste of the pro tour, hit 75 mph on a bass boat, and nearly saw two legends throw down on the water. The only thing I didn't do was catch a lot of fish. I had only a couple of dinky ones in the boat and finished the first day way down in the amateur standings.

School Stays in Session

The second day, I fished with Cliff Kraft. Nice guy who gave me a pretty mediocre day. I put another couple in my live well, but nothing spectacular. But Day Three was a different story. I drew David Fritts, who was possibly the best crankbait fisherman around. Just like I did with Tommy Biffle, I spent the day watching him, observing his crankbait technique. I was totally blown away, loving his approach, the way he was covering water and constantly moving. Fritts gave me more exposure to power fishing, which would eventually become my style. He even caught two fish on both sides of a treble hook, which I had never seen before. (I've done it maybe a dozen times since, but at the time, it was amazing to see two fish snagged on one lure.)

I also noticed he didn't watch his rod tip. He just looked around, leaning his whippy fiberglass rod on his leg. I had no clue what he was up to, but was very intrigued. I later learned he was purposely delaying his reaction to strikes, so he wouldn't set the hook too fast. In crankbait fishing, you want that fish to engulf the bait before setting the hook. It's really easy to pull the lure away from the fish too quickly. By not focusing on his rod tip, Fritts was forcing himself to go strictly by feel. Using a fiberglass rod, which isn't as sensitive as graphite, helped deaden the vibrations transmitted when a fish hits the lure, which he desensitized even more by putting the rod against his leg. This gave that fish more time to eat the bait.

But as good as fishing with Fritts was, my last day was totally amazing. I drew Gary Klein, who was a complete machine out there. I had never seen anyone so proficient using time management in his fishing. Cast in, cast out. He was incredibly accurate and had an unbelievable look in his eyes that said "all business." As impressive as the other three guys were, I was most impressed by Gary Klein. It's weird. There's nobody on tour I respect more than Gary Klein, and it started that day in North Carolina. Yet some people think we're rivals, since I beat him in the '03 Classic. Whatever. If I have half the career Gary has had, I'll consider myself lucky.

Winning for Losing

By my standards, I really bombed out in that tournament, finishing forty-third. No excuses about it being my first pro-am, or not knowing the water. All that mattered was that I didn't win, or even come close. But the experience was incredibly valuable, and so was my mediocre finish. A Top 10 showing would have convinced me everything I was doing was money, which would have masked weaknesses that needed fixing. Instead, I was humbled and put in my place, realizing I didn't know everything. I got back to Runnemede and was fired up. All I wanted to do was learn, and I had a body of new information and practical knowledge that I *could not wait* to use. I wanted to get out on Alloway Lake and try what Tommy Biffle was doing with jigs or lie a whippy rod on my leg without looking at the tip, just like David Fritts had. I was absolutely desperate to experience everything those pros did.

JERKBAITS

At the 1999 Vermont Top 150 at Lake Champlain, a nasty cold front came through before the final day, lowering the water temperature like an ice bath. I had been fishing for largemouth, but the water temperature shut them down. On Champlain, however, those same conditions activate the smallmouth. So I took out my jerkbait and was able to pull enough weight to hold off Rick Clunn for my first major victory. Jerkbaits fit perfectly into my power-fishing style. I can use them to cover a huge amount of water and generate great reaction strikes. Another bonus? Jerkbaits are one of the few lures that work well year-round. But to use them effectively, you need to remember a few things.

CADENCE. The rhythm you choose to move your lure is the key to jerkbait fishing. It's different from day to day, hour to hour, on each body of water. One way of finding it is by picking your favorite song and imitating its beat in your retrieve. Jerk, jerk, pause. Jerk, jerk, pause. If rhythm doesn't attract them, pick another song. Jerk, pause, jerk. Jerk, pause, jerk. Don't forget to change your pause rates, too. Sometimes it's just a quickie, sometimes a super long stop. In general, colder water needs a longer pause, and vice versa. Homing in on the right cadence requires concentration and attention, but once you get the hang of it, jerkbaits will fill up your live well.

SEASONALITY. I divide jerkbaits into three categories: floating, suspending, and sinking. There are key times of year to use each.

Pre-spawn to Post-spawn. This is my favorite time for jerkbaits. The water is still cool and the fish are lethargic, so I'll use a suspending bait, something that stays in the strike zone longer and looks like an easy meal. A lure that imitates a dying shad is a natural choice for winter. I tend to pick up my cadence and shorten the pauses.

Summertime. Summer can be a tough period for jerkbaits, because fish tend to go deep into vegetation as the water heats up, and jerkbaits aren't ideal in thick cover. But that doesn't mean they can't be thrown at all. A floating jerkbait, which rises to the top and has a little more side-to-side action, entices active fish to strike. I like to use a pearl blue back model to imitate alewife or herring, or a clown color that resembles yellow perch. Bass will set up shop in locations like current breaks and eddies, waiting for a meal to drift by, so hit the shoals, flats, headwaters, and creeks.

Wintertime. Winter's a great time to use sinking jerkbaits, also called countdown minnows. These lures are phenomenal for getting down into those lower-depth zones where fish often hang out. I like a sinking rate of about a foot a second. Remember, wintertime jerkbaiting requires patience. Count down to your depth, give it a couple of twitches, *and let it sit!* That's the key. My pause lengths can go well over thirty seconds, as ridiculous as that may sound, because during winter, many forage species are dying from the cold conditions, and that's what you need to imitate.

TACKLE AND EQUIPMENT. I like a rod with similar properties to a crankbait rod. The fiberglass composite lets me delay the hook-set and load up on the tip for maximum casting distance. Choose a shorter rod like the six-foot LT Series model S from Team Daiwa for the higher wrist action that's so crucial to twitching a jerkbait. The reel should have a large spool cast and average retrieve speed. Line is super critical, because it affects depth control. I like green Berkley Trilene and Berkley Vanish line in 6- to 12-pound test. Another great way to adjust your sink or suspend rate is by modifying hook sizes or adding weighted golf tape to the belly's underside.

9 WHERE YOU GONNA PARK THAT THING?

Lake Norman, vol. II

In my first pro-am, at Lake Norman in North Carolina in the fall of '92, I finished 43rd. It felt a lot worse, though. To me, there's no difference between 43rd and 143rd. I left with a taste of the life, but wanted to do better, so I put in deposits to fish every pro-am of the '93–'94 season. Oddly enough, I drew Lake Norman again, scheduled for May of '94.

This was a chance for revenge on the fishery that had beaten me the year before. And since they made the drawings in the fall of '93, I had over six months to think about the tournament and get ready, using tactics I learned from those pros. I had insight into the lake's forage, so it was easier for me to "match the hatch" with my lure choices. By the time May rolled around, I was fully prepared. This time, I went to Lake Norman fishing not to learn, but to win. Not just the tournament, but the grand prize on the amateur side, a brand-new Ranger 374 bass boat with a Johnson 150-hp motor on the back, and a trailer to tow it. I was still stuck in my little twelve-foot johnboat and didn't have the money to step up and buy a bigger boat. I had no intention of leaving North Carolina without that Ranger.

When I got to Mooresville, everything from meeting my partners to getting a hotel to registration felt more comfortable than it had in '92. I was still green, for sure, but not in awe like the first time around. Every moment I was there I grew more confident I could win. Only one thing was left—the fishing gods had to partner me with guys who would be around the fish. As an amateur, I was fishing out of the back of the boat, and was completely at the mercy of the pro. I go where he goes, fish what he fishes. If the pro isn't on the fish, the amateur is screwed. So at the meeting before the tournament, as they were calling out names I was whispering, "C'mon, c'mon, c'mon, let me get a good one. . . ."

Runnemede, New Jersey, and Suwannee, Georgia. Mike Iaconelli and Cliff Kraft."

I immediately flashed back to '92, when Cliff and I were paired up and had a pretty weak day. Cliff is a great angler, but the memories of the last tournament meant I wasn't excited to ride with him again. I thought, "First day of the tournament, and I'm with some dude who ain't gonna catch anything." By the end of the day, I owed Cliff Kraft an apology, because he had me on fish all day. I was flipping a green pumpkin–style jig under docks, just like Tommy Biffle had when I rode with him, and brought in three solid keepers. Unfortunately, I also lost one and missed another, which I kept replaying in my head. I've always had a tendency to beat myself up over mistakes, and this was no exception. I figured those fish would cost me the tournament, and didn't even bother checking the standings. But at dinner that night, my uncle Don showed up all excited because I was within five pounds of first! Not bad at all! There was plenty of time to make that up. All of a sudden, I was thinking "W" again!

Day Two

Going into Day Two I knew my partner would be Carl Maxfield. I was excited to fish with him, because I really believed Carl would be right on 'em. All night, I dreamed about what I'd do back out on the water, focusing on my rod position and how I'd keep it aimed at one o'clock, with the butt end square against my ribs on every cast, working off feel.

My hunch about Carl was dead-on. From moment one, we were on the fish, and I had one of those magical days. I was totally in the zone. Every time I made a choice between my rod and lure combinations, it was the perfect one. I pulled in three keepers with a Stone Jig, and two more with a spinnerbait and topwater popper. I even got to cull once. That I was using different techniques only made it sweeter. Even then, versatility was important to me. In the meantime, up front, Carl was upset because he wasn't catching them. Very few things frustrate a pro more—myself included—than an amateur smoking him from the back of the boat. But I didn't care, because I was on fire! Going into the weigh-in, I figured five fish would push me way up in the standings, and I was right. I shot from twenty-first to third, only a pound and a half out of first place.

Fishing with Guido

I felt great going into the third day, and not just because I had a good shot at winning that Ranger, but because I'd drawn Guido Hibdon. He was in the Top 10 on the pro side, so I knew he'd be all business. Even better, he went out of his way to tell me exactly what he'd be doing the next day, so I could prepare. He knew I was in contention and offered encouragement, almost making me feel like we were a team. "C'mon, we're gonna get you some fish. You're gonna do real good in this tournament!" Obviously, he'd still be running the show, but his attitude made me feel great, and boosted my confidence. I had been on a great jig pattern, so when Guido told me we'd do about an hour of topwater, then hit docks all day, I was totally stoked. It was perfect for my pattern. I knew he'd be fishing a little worm, so I decided to stay on the jig and reach some places he couldn't instead of rolling over spots he'd just hit.

I could barely sleep that night, and when I finally got out on the water, I was absolutely wired. So jacked, in fact, that I managed to bury a treble hook into my palm. That was the first time I'd ever been hooked, but my adrenaline was pumping so hard, I just grabbed my pliers, and *rip!* I tore the hook right out and kept casting, rubbing off the blood running down my hands. It didn't even faze me. Guido thought I was nuts. That, by the way, is *not* how you're supposed to remove a hook.

Four hours later, my optimism was gone. I had nothing. My thoughts turned ugly again. "Here goes the day. Two hours left, and I'm screwed!" Then it hit me like a ton of bricks. While we had been flipping these docks, trying to get way back under, I kept seeing these big balls of shad swimming together in schools. Not underneath, but *between* the docks. It finally registered! I went into my bag and pulled out a Fin-S Fish, a fairly new lure that looked exactly like those schooling shad. First cast, *Rrrhhhhoooom!* My first keeper! Money! In just an hour and a half, I caught two more good ones. Then, right at the wire, I caught a fourth to finish the day. It wasn't a limit, but I was proud of myself for adapting to the environment and picking up on something even a seasoned pro like Guido missed. Weighing in felt even better, since my bag was enough to bump me into first place, a pound and a half ahead of the field!

The icing on the cake came when Guido weighed in and told the crowd I was a heck of a fisherman and too good to be an amateur. He talked me up big-time. It's impossible to describe how it felt hearing someone of Guido's stature compliment me like that. When we got to the parking lot, he even asked me for a couple of my Fin-S Fish. Every pro knows how insecure amateurs can be, and often will still treat them badly. Guido didn't do that. Even after Cliff had warned him that I was pretty aggressive, Guido treated me with respect, almost like we were colleagues. He taught me more about how a pro should treat his amateur partner than anyone I've ever fished with.

So Close I Can Taste It

I was one good bag away from hauling that Ranger boat home and taking the next huge step in my fishing career. My Day Four draw was Chet Douthit, which was great, because he wanted to fish the exact pattern Guido and I had done the day before. In my mind, that was a perfect plan, and I was right. Chet and I went out and freakin' destroyed them. Destroyed them! Both of us were so deep in the zone, we didn't say a word to each other all day. Chet was throwing a spinnerbait, and I was right behind with a Fin-S Fish. I had my polarized sunglasses on, scanning between the docks for little dark spots—stumps submerged in the water. I knew the fish would be around them, and by finding their exact spots I didn't have to do blind casts—and the bass would just fly off them onto the lure, all day long. I must have landed ten keepers from the back of the boat. That's unheard of! I culled my way up to the biggest amateur weight of the tournament, and ended up blowing away the field. In fact, my total weight of 24.1 pounds would have put me in the Top 25 among the pros. It was an amazing result.

All in the Family

I remember coming off the stage and seeing my family totally stoked. Pop was off to the side, and I could see how proud he was. Seeing him that happy made it even sweeter, you know? I had this big trophy, and then they handed me the keys to the boat. My new Ranger! For the first time, the media was all over me, and the whole scene was just crazy. But I couldn't figure out how we'd get the boat home. Then my family again proved that they're my biggest fans and supporters. I learned they were so confident in me that while I was out fishing that last day, my uncle Don ran down to Pep Boys, spent a few hundred bucks, and had a Class 3 hitch installed on his van to tow the Ranger (that I hadn't won yet) back home. If I hadn't had a great day, he might as well have burned his money, since Don had no use for a hitch. When I won, I couldn't figure out how we'd get the boat home . . . then Don told me what he'd done. That was so cool!

After it was over, I went to the parking lot and sat in the boat, trying to comprehend that it was mine. And I'll never forget what happened next. Kevin VanDam walked by, and we made eye contact. And he gave me this look that said, "I'll see you again. Welcome to the club." It was mind blowing. When I got back to New Jersey, I spent hours looking in every compartment of the boat, and later that night, I actually slept in it! No blanket, no covers, nothing! Just a spring night in Jersey, and the happiest angler in the world sprawled out across the bench seat of his new Ranger.

Driver's Ed

Winning that boat was huge, and it meant that I had a chance to take the next step up the ladder from club fishing to the Federation level (run by BASS) and the Red Man circuit, run by the FLW (Red Mans are now called BFL tournaments). The regional Federation was BASS's grassroots organization, and with a lot of success, an angler could even make the Classic through that circuit. As for the Red Man Tournament Trail, success there could land you in the All-American, a pretty important tournament in its own right. I was ready for the challenge but made a conscious decision to wait a year to make the leap. Some things had to be taken care of first. Just like with a car, you have to work out a new bass boat's engine before going full throttle, or you risk blowing it up. But more important, I wanted to take the time to learn how to properly use it in the first place. Good thing, too, since I learned quickly that driv-

MODERNIZING BOATS

In the early years, professional anglers were running john-boats, the same ragged tubs I used with Top Rod. But everything changed in the late 1960s, when a few small companies started making modern bass boats. Of those, Ranger Boats, founded by Forrest L. Wood, was the most important. Wood was like the Henry Ford of bass boats. It started out almost as a hobby, creating boats for a few local anglers (including some for Ray Scott's first BASS tournaments), but by the early 1970s, Ranger had started mass-producing true bass boats with live wells, bigger outboards, hydraulic steering, and foot-controlled motors. They were cheap, too, with some models costing under a thousand dollars. Since that time, boats have gone through huge changes, including horsepower restrictions. When I started fishing, you couldn't have an outboard larger than 150 horsepower. As boats started getting bigger, 150 rose to 200, which rose to 250, so the boats could be safely controlled. Prices shot up too. A top-of-the-line boat can top out near $50,000!

ing a bass boat wasn't quite the same as ripping around Runnemede in my Toyota pickup.

The first time I drove it was on the Delaware River with Kristi, at a launch called Hardgroves. Right away, I was nervous because I had no clue what I was doing, and the current at the landing really moved. The first thing I found out was that Kristi hated being in the boat. She was completely freaked out, and who can blame her? I was cruising outside the channel markers! You're supposed to stay right of the red posts, left of the green. I didn't know that, until this dude started frantically waving at me, yelling, "You can't run there! The water's not deep enough!

Stay within the channel." No problem. . . . What's a channel? I must have been out there eight hours without dropping a line, just getting the hang of the electronics, the throttle, and how everything worked. I really felt like I was getting it, until I tried putting the boat back on the trailer. As I was getting it secured, the current pushed it against the dock, popping a tennis ball–size hole in the gunnel. I was so mad! My baby, the most amazing thing I'd ever owned, and I popped a hole in it on the first day! I nearly cried. But there was a silver lining. I knew right away I wouldn't be an "anal angler," a guy who is so uptight about his boat's appearance that he won't take it anywhere it might get scratched or scraped, which limits opportunity. Aggressiveness and pushing equipment has helped me become the angler I am today. I doubt I would have ended up an "anal angler," but at least now I could test the boat's limits, since I'd already guaranteed it wouldn't stay pristine.

BOAT POSITIONING

Oftentimes anglers get so keyed up on their lure choices and plan of attack for fishing their sweet spots that they never consider how to position the boat when they get there. Boat positioning may be the most overlooked aspect of bass fishing, and it's easily one of the most important. Having your boat in the wrong spot makes it that much harder to find the ideal casting angles. Plus, mishandling your boat might spook the fish or cloud the water before you've even thrown a single cast.

I have two big goals as I position my boat. The first is maximizing my cast's effectiveness. Before each cast, I think about the angle I want to present the lure, and how to bring the fish out after it's hooked, visualizing that connection between my location and the target. The second is to create a "safe zone" that minimizes my impact on the environment and keeps those bass in a biting mood. It changes constantly, depending on water clarity, current, wind, and light conditions, and dictates how I use my electronics and trolling motor. There are countless variables, but also some general rules of thumb.

- Position yourself for longer casts in clearer water.
- Avoid hitting the bank or cover with the boat.
- Always cast upstream when there is current present.
- Always keep your trolling motor at a constant speed, and whenever possible, simply let the wind or current take you in the direction you want. That said, watch your drift. Currents can easily pull you away from ideal angles.

Using positioning aides makes life easier. I frequently mark my position using my Lowrance GPS while surveying a lake and establishing my pattern, so I can pinpoint sweet spots and find them efficiently later on. Had I not been careful about my GPS points in the Louisiana Delta in '03, I might have never found my winning area.

Other tools can help maximize your boat positioning: Drop buoy markers. Use drifting aides. Wind socks help fight strong winds and help keep your boat in place without draining battery power, which make them great in drift situations.

Learn to use your boat and navigation equipment properly, and you'll have an advantage the competition probably won't recognize.

10 BACK TO SCHOOL

Rowan University

People always tell me, "It was so smart to learn advertising and marketing in college." And it's true. I learned so much at school about marketing myself, how to appear in front of a camera, and the value of exposure. People assume I chose that major for a future fishing career, but honestly, when I got to Rowan, I still hadn't made that leap of faith to become a professional fisherman. In the beginning, I figured my classes would help me more in my DJ business than fishing. Or I figured I'd just be an ad guy, someday writing copy at a good firm.

Unlike high school, I took Rowan very seriously. I had never been more motivated academically, and I give most of the credit to Rowan's fantastic marketing program. Senior year, they divided the marketing majors into groups, and we had to solicit a company, design an advertising campaign from start to finish, and present it to them. My group worked with Ace, a job placement service for physically handicapped people, so we created a campaign convincing people that despite being disabled, the handicapped make excellent hires. It wasn't the most exciting campaign in the world, but the process was really interesting, and I learned a lot. More important, working that assignment and other really cool ones we did made the possibility of working in the ad world seem exciting. In the meantime, I had stepped up from club tournaments, and was getting more competitive on the Federation and Red Man circuits, but still hadn't committed to the idea of going pro. In my heart I wanted it, but I knew how hard it'd be. Then there was my relationship with Kristi, which, after several periods of being on and off, was going great. She wasn't comfortable with fishing's unstable lifestyle, and I didn't want to rock the boat.

Ike the Intern

Advertising and marketing majors were required to do an internship during the second semester of senior year. I really liked writing copy during the Ace campaign and thought being a lead copywriter for an ad firm would be pretty sweet. So I was excited to land an internship at Pellone and Sweeney in Mount Laurel, learning the ropes under an ad exec, five days a week, like a regular corporate Joe. And just like I did while fishing with experts, I asked the A.E. tons of questions. He was a really cool dude, but his answers scared the hell out of me. He'd already been there two or three years, and was still, more or less, a glorified coffee boy. Worse, he would probably have to wait another six or seven years before getting his shot at being a lead copywriter. Ten years? That's what it took before you were in that lead position on ad campaigns? Until then, that's ten years of putting on a suit, fighting traffic, and getting people coffee. I'd still be doing it as we speak! That's a ton of coffee, you know?

Plus, I was really starting to pump up my fishing. All through '95, I was only fishing Top Rod and other local club tournaments. But now that I'd had some success on the Red Man and Federation circuits, and had a legitimate shot to step up even higher, I had to weigh my options—coffee boy, DJ, or bass fisherman? Java delivery quickly got axed. I knew in my heart that I didn't want to get pigeonholed into some stereotypical cubicle hell. As for deejaying, that may be the one way on the planet to make a living that's *less* stable than bass fishing. I was making three hundred dollars a night under the table as a college student, but to earn a good living was seriously tough. Parties come and go, and I watched so many DJ's fall to the wayside. Bass fishing actually seemed more legitimate in comparison. So that was it. I decided to dedicate myself fully to becoming a professional angler. I knew my family would support me, since I now had a degree to fall back on. There was only one more person to tell.

She didn't handle the news well.

*B*reaking Up Again

When I told Kristi in the summer of '96 that I was going to try fishing professionally, we split up. It wasn't a huge blowout or anything. She basically just said, "I'm out." In hindsight, I understand why she was upset. I was still living with my uncle, and she was at home. I had worked my butt off to finish school, which she waited patiently for me to do, and now I was blowing off my degree to be a professional fisherman? We were both into our twenties, and she wanted a bigger commitment and a more secure future. I think she thought the real issue was that I didn't want to grow up, period.

Kristi breaking up with me really scrambled my brain. I had finally made the very difficult decision to become a professional fisherman and it blew up in my face. I was torn between following my heart and choosing the girl and the stable nine-to-five life. But I kept thinking of myself wearing a suit and fighting traffic just to deliver coffee. I didn't want to do it. So there I was, in August of '96, with a four-year degree, no job, and a five-year relationship down the tubes. I was totally confused. So I did what anyone in my situation would have done.

I went right back to school.

I decided to get my teaching certificate, figuring that would be the best compromise. It was a real, legitimate job I thought I'd enjoy, and I'd have summers off to fish Federation and Red Man tournaments. Teaching was the best of both worlds. I wouldn't be a professional fisherman, but I'd still be competing while maintaining a real job, and I'd be happy. And in the back of my mind, I hoped this would keep fishing from screwing up my next relationship. So in the fall of '96, I was accepted into the postbaccalaureate program at Rowan to get my teaching certificate. I was that dude on the freakin' ten-year program, you know?

Good-bye, Pop . . .

I wish the worst thing that happened to me that year was breaking up with Kristi. It wasn't. Not even close. In 1996, Pop died of a stroke. He had lived a long, full life, for which we were all grateful. But after 85 years of life, his body was worn out. He had been dealing with full-blown emphysema and Parkinson's disease, so we all knew what was coming, but that didn't bring much comfort when my mom gave me the news. I was absolutely devastated. I had never dealt with a loss like that. A few friends of mine had passed away already, but never someone I was this close to. At first, I was in denial, saying to myself, "Nope, it didn't happen." I don't know why, but it's always been my nature to deal with emotional events by myself rather than opening up to my family. So after the initial denial period ended, I locked myself in my room for the whole night, just dealing with my pain alone in a pitch-black room. That was my therapy.

Pop had played such a huge role in my life. He was more of a father figure than a grandfather, the head of a family unit that spent their entire lives no further than five minutes apart. While lots of kids are lucky to see their grandfather a couple of times a year, I had lived with him until I was almost thirteen. He was so instrumental to my fishing career, and was the main reason I picked up a rod in the first place. His father taught him, he taught my uncle, and they both taught me. I became a bass fisherman the minute I snuck that Rapala out of his box, even though I didn't know it yet. During our trips to the Poconos, he constantly talked me up, going out of his way to tell the world every time I caught a limit of trout. And when I won that boat in 1994 at Lake Norman, my whole family was happy, but Pop was glowing like a neon light.

The last time I saw him was at his house the weekend before he died. At that point, he was basically restricted to the house, watching TV, trying to eat, taking the occasional trip to the store with my uncle. He looked bad, but I just wanted to take his mind off his deteriorating health. We had our normal conversation, which meant a lot of talk about fishing. We acted like nothing was wrong, even though we both knew the end was coming. He never got overly emotional, and I always go back to the Fred Sanford comparison. You always knew what Fred was feeling, even if he never admitted it. I knew how much Pop loved me and how proud I made him. He didn't need to say anything.

My first win after he passed away came a few years later, at Lake Champlain in 1999. I dedicated the victory to him onstage, saying, "This is for my grandfather." And when I won the Classic, I definitely felt his presence. It's funny, because I saw my mom, uncle, and grandmom out in the audience and they were all animated and visibly excited. But I know Pop would have stayed cool, like he knew all along I'd win. Old-school guys don't freak out, scream "Oh my God, that was amazing!" and start hugging everyone, even though deep down he would have liked to. But I would have known.

Back with Kristi . . . Again

I barely got going in my teaching program before I knew I wasn't going to be happy. I knew in my heart what I wanted to do, and finally came to terms with it. I had tried all these avenues, working at Accumark, advertising, teaching, and didn't have a passion for any of them. Ultimately, every experience led back to the same place. I wanted to be a professional bass fisherman. My mind was made up, and the only issue left was Kristi. I had spent a year living with my buddy Brian, partying nonstop, scoring girls, and doing all the things I felt like I missed out on when I was with Kristi, but in the end I still loved her and I knew she loved me. I wanted to get back together with her, but I wasn't willing to sacrifice my dream to do it, so I sat her down and laid everything on the table. She *had* to be okay with my fishing career, or it was no deal. This time, I wasn't compromising, I wasn't going back to school, I wasn't going to the ad agency. I was willing to toss the relationship if need be. I said, "This is how it's gonna be. If you have any problems with it, I need to know now." I guess by then Kristi really understood how important fishing was to me, and how serious I was about succeeding. She wanted me to be happy, and, like me, thought we could make it work. So she said, "Go for it. Follow your dreams." Kristi was all in, and so was I. Mike Iaconelli would become a pro fisherman.

SO YOU WANT TO GO PRO? THE BLUEPRINT

Think you're ready to take on me, Kevin VanDam, Denny Brauer, and Skeet Reese, week in and week out? You need to understand what you're getting into, or you'll find yourself in a world of trouble. There are tons of issues that dictate how well you'll do on the BASS or FLW tours before you've even dropped a lure in the water.

HOW GOOD IS GOOD ENOUGH? To make it on tour, you have to be really, really, *really* good, or you'll get run off the water. That means consistency. You can't just dominate your home water but bomb everywhere else. I saw lots of that coming up through the Federation in New Jersey. I remember this guy Skip, who dominated at Lake Hopatcong. He'd just crush! But throw him on the Hudson, the Delaware, or the Potomac, and he'd never per- form. If you're consistent and succeed outside your home court advantage, that's a sign you're ready. Technique + Versatility = Consistency!

DON'T SKIP ANY STEPS. I'm a huge believer in climbing the ladder without skipping steps. Start in your local club, then grow into the Federations and BFLs (Bass Fishing League), and finally the Opens and EverStarts (a semipro level) before hitting the big time. Skipping steps will screw you. It happened to my Top Rod buddy Chris. He won a couple of Club Classics, was our angler of the year, and had more talent than half the guys on tour right now. But he tried jumping straight into the semi-pros, got in over his head, and his skills couldn't make up for it. Take your time and pace yourself. It will happen when you're ready!

CHECK YOUR BANK ACCOUNT. A lot of people don't realize that fishing just one pro circuit, either BASS or FLW, means $40,000-$50,000 in expenses. Lodging. Gas. Food. Gear. Clothing (everything from subarctic Gore-Tex to zip-off shorts for broiling hot July days). You'll probably need a boat, don't you think? Another forty grand, minimum. A honkin' tow vehicle (like my Suburban). It's thirty or forty grand more, especially when you toss in maintenance and wear. So let's say you hit the FLW Tour, take fiftieth in one event, twenty-fifth in another—not bad for a start. Congratulations, you've made $30,000 . . . except you could be $80,000 in the hole! Which brings me to . . .

YOU HAVE TO WANT THIS. Fishing professionally means more than just going out to fish. It's a business, and a hard one at that. You're taking on a lifestyle that pulls you away from your wife, kids, and any roots at home. Up at 4:30 A.M. and asleep by 11 P.M. every day for four weeks straight. It gets to the point where it goes from "Am I good enough to do this?" to "Do I really *want* to do this?" Fishing must be your passion. Your life. Yeah, you might make it big, but in between it's forty thousand miles a year on the road, living out of a suitcase in bad motels, and eating worse meals. Bottom line? You must live for the feeling of fooling fish with artificial lures. The desire to conquer a hundred thousand lakes you've never been to and piece together an endless puzzle. Unless that urgency to be the best angler alive lives within you, you'd better pick a different profession.

Shoe salesman, anyone?

11 MY LAST REGULAR JOB

Mike the Fishing Manager

Even with my decision to go pro, I still needed a job. Deejaying was out, because I was fishing tournaments every weekend. In Federation events, tournaments were on Sundays, with practice on Saturday, and the Red Man circuit had Saturday competitions, with Thursday and Friday practices. So unless people started throwing major parties on Mondays and Tuesdays, I wouldn't make much cash spinning. I needed a job that paid well and still let me pursue a fishing career, and I wasn't sure where I'd find it, until I headed one afternoon up to Dick's Sporting Goods in Mount Laurel, like I'd done a thousand times before. But this time, there was a sign on the door. POSITIONS AVAILABLE IN HUNTING AND FISHING. I was intrigued. I've always believed in signs, things happening to point you in the right direction. Well, this was *literally* a sign pointing me in the right direction.

So I filled out an application to work in the fishing department. My first interview was with the assistant manager, a guy named Jessie. We were having a great conversation, and I could tell he thought I was qualified. But he never asked me anything about fishing, which was strange. It wasn't until about halfway through that I realized he wanted to hire me in operations, which is a fancy name for shipping and receiving. Accumark with sporting goods? Hell no! I told him about the mix-up, and he set up an appointment with Ed Nailor, the manager of the Lodge (what Dick's calls their hunting and fishing departments) to interview for "Fishing Lead," the fishing department manager. Ken Klodnicki, who managed the hunting department, was also there. These are great guys, but they had nothing beyond a basic knowledge of fishing, so they asked simple questions. "What does a depth finder do? What is the difference between a bait caster and a spin caster?" The way their jaws hit the floor after my answers, you'd have thought I was Stephen Hawking! Ed stopped the interview and said, "This is stupid. You're hired." Assuming, of course, that the store manager, Mike Biaggi, liked me.

I walked into his office.

"So, I hear you fish."

"Yeah."

Biaggi smiled wide. "I used to do a little fishing in my time."

Sometimes I think I've lived a charmed life. This was one of those times. My "interview" turned into an hour-long bull session about fishing. Mike was a pioneer of the New Jersey Federation program, an avid fisherman who once aspired to go pro but held off for family reasons or something. So the store manager was a hard-core fisherman who followed the sport, and more important, understood how my goals in fishing would affect my work schedule. I wouldn't just need weekends off for tournaments. I'd sometimes need a whole week off to travel to event venues for practice. Mike told me that assuming I took care of business at the store, he was okay with my freaky scheduling needs. Maybe because he didn't have a chance to live out his dream, he wanted to help me live mine. I'm not sure. But by the end of the summer of '97, I was the fishing department manager at Dick's Sporting Goods. Forty-hour workweek, pretty good money, and I had a foot in the fishing industry. But even with those perks, I still had no idea how important that job would be.

Dick's Gets Ike-ified

Over the next few months, I started loving my job. People would arrive totally clueless about fishing, and I'd help them walk out with good gear without putting one over on anyone. I loved that I could do that. Eventually, when I started doing well in the Federation and Red Man events, people who knew I worked there would bring in maps for me to break down. Ed had to remind me more than once that I was there to sell product, not be a fishing oracle for the tristate area. It was okay, though, because most of the time people would leave with something, and I brought a lot of people into the store. It was a win-win situation for everyone.

Our managers gave me and Ken a lot of leeway in the Lodge. If the customers responded positively, and it helped move product, we could try just about anything. When I got to Dick's, all the fishing gear was laid out in a confusing mash. Saltwater and bass fishing lures were mixed together. Bass and fly rods, too. Anglers want all their artificials in one spot, all their fly stuff in another spot, and so on. I became obsessed with reorganizing my section in a more logical way. I also started leaning on Ed and Mike to carry higher-end product. I knew it would sell, since we were in a neighborhood filled with avid fishermen, many of whom were fairly well off. My managers may have started off skeptical, but once they saw product moving, they were fully on board.

I quickly learned that people were more likely to buy gear if they could see its effectiveness firsthand. So I started cutting the hooks off lures and casting in the aisles. I'd throw them at strange angles and drill hard-to-reach targets with pinpoint accuracy. People were blown away by these shows, and would often buy what I was using. During downtime we would string up targets around the Lodge and take aim: "Who can hit the box of clay pigeons first? Who can ding the hunting hat on the left?" It eventually got to be like that old McDonald's commercial with Larry Bird and Michael Jordan, where they played that outrageous game of horse. "Off the rafters, off the scoreboard, off the backboard, all net." Except, for us, it was "Off the deer decoy, around the fly rods, over the sale bin, all net." One time, I remember pitching this brown, skirted jig across the floor, and a woman started screaming, "A mouse! A mouse!" She had lungs, too! Other times we'd be pitching down an aisle, and someone would turn in to the lure while it was airborne. We'd have to yank it back really quick and apologize.

It started out as an excuse to screw around in the store, but I saw my technique and accuracy improve dramatically. I was throwing every cast in the book for almost three years. I even became proficient with both hands, which is rare among anglers, in large part from working at Dick's. By the time I left, I could drill a BB target from halfway across the store. I was Annie Oakley with a rod.

Improving my skills wasn't the only fringe benefit of my job at Dick's. I also was able to get gear at cost, which is incredibly important for a struggling Federation angler. Plus, I knew when things would go on sale, so I would pull stock that I'd eventually buy myself. I was like a kid in a candy store. When we'd get a new shipment of lures like rattle-traps, I'd grab my favorite colors, then go through each one, shaking them to find the lures with the loudest rattle. Then I'd put them in my "to buy" pile before customers ever saw them. How sick is that? And even though I was low on the Dick's Sporting Goods totem pole, through my managerial duties, I was making connections with all the equipment company reps and meeting some important heavy hitters in the industry, helping me build foundations for future relationships. Dick's was the beginning of my industry education.

My Eyes, They Don't See So Good

I worked at Dick's right when the Jerky Boys—those dudes who'd crank-call people randomly—were at their most popular. I had all their fake voices down cold, but my favorite was Saul Rosenberg, this old dude who would call up different businesses and complain about everything. He'd drive people crazy! Well, one day I discovered that the phone system at work had a feature that allowed you to call any other Dick's store with the press of a button. So, randomly, Ken and I would call other stores. I'd have some poor dude running all over looking for products that didn't exist, or thinking a totally irate customer was coming in to ream him out. It was great! I'd use that Saul Rosenberg voice and ask infuriating questions, like "What do you feed the clay pigeons? Do you have parachute pants?" After a while, other employees caught on to what Ken and I were doing, and there'd be a huge crowd of people watching us mess with other stores. Even Ed, my freakin' manager, got in on it!

Occasionally, though, my smooth sailing at Dick's would hit a wrinkle, and Bad Ike would come out for a visit. One afternoon, the Lodge was just packed. Everyone and their mother was shopping, and I was the only guy scheduled. Ken had left Dick's by then, so all of a sudden I had hunting responsibilities on top of fishing. I didn't know jack about hunting! I was afraid to touch any of that stuff and accidentally blow my head off. All these people kept asking me questions I couldn't answer, and the customers were getting terrible service. After my shift, I snapped. I took my pink card, a license to sell firearms in the state of New Jersey, which every manager had to have, and tore it into about a billion pieces, yelling, "I'm not selling that stuff anymore!" I may be the only person in the history of Dick's to shred his pink card. It was a monumental freak-out that would have gotten any other employee canned. I went in the next day and apologized to Mike Biaggi. I was shocked (and thankful) that he forgave me. And I never got another pink card, either. I guess I won't be opening a firearms shop anytime soon.

But it's not only *off* the water that my intensity gets me in trouble. The same drive that pushes me to the next level when things are going good, like it did on Lake Norman or the Louisiana Delta in '03, can also kick me in the butt when things are going wrong. I've broken rods, cursed myself and everyone around me, and basically behaved like a baby. At an E50 event (this series was introduced during the 2004 season. It consists of four no-entry-fee tournaments, with every angler walking away with a minimum of twenty grand for the series) in '04 on the Alabama River, I broke off two casts in a row, including a four-pound spotted bass right next to the boat. My response was a little less than Zen-like. I took my reel, a three-hundred-dollar piece of equipment, and threw it as far up the river as I could. My amateur was just floored! I saw him again at the FLW Championship, and he said, "Mike, that was the funniest freakin' thing I've ever seen in my entire life." Glad one of us was amused.

12 LIFESTYLES OF THE POOR AND NOT FAMOUS

Time Share

Fishing is a rough lifestyle, especially when you're working your way up the ladder. Time is a constant issue, especially for guys with families. Until my ex and I split, everything was always about time lines. Scheduling enough practice to feel confident on the water, but still leaving enough time at home. Fishing a tournament for eight hours, then jumping in the truck and booking it home so I didn't miss another minute with my kids. Everything takes time. Packing the truck. Doing map study and research. It takes at least a day to tie on all the baits. Packing the right tackle. Loading up the Suburban with the microwave, the clothes bag, and all the backup gear. There just aren't enough hours in the day.

Get Your Motor Running!

But those hectic days at home are a cakewalk compared to life on the road. Even for regional tournaments, it can take ten hours to reach a fishery. In the pros, that can jump to twenty. You drive like a madman to get there, try to settle in, and have a full day of fishing the next day. Everything's "Go! Go! Go!" You are literally Mad Max, a road warrior moving from event to event, come hell or high water. I've driven through hurricanes, rain, snow, and golf ball–size hail that left spider cracks in my windshield. And try steering a Suburban through a blowout with a two-thousand-pound boat attached to the back. It's happened to me maybe a dozen times, and let me tell you, it ain't easy. My only advice: don't hit what's in front of you and don't get killed. The amount of abuse you put on your truck in mileage and wear is unbelievable. You can destroy your ride without even knowing it. One time, I was heading down to Lake Seminole, really pushing myself, because after fifteen hours I wanted out of that car. At about 2 A.M. I finally reached Jack Wingate's, a lodge down by the lake. I was off-my-rocker delirious, and passed out the moment I hit the bed. The next morning, as I was walking to my truck, I noticed that one of the wheels on my double-axle boat trailer was gone! Gone! It could have fallen off in New Jersey, and I went another thousand miles short a tire. It could have flown to the side of the road and killed a pedestrian. I have no idea. When you're Mad Max, insanity is par for the course.

The Presidential Suite . . . Not!

Early on, in my Federation and Red Man days, I created homes away from home in the worst dive hotels, motels, and lodges imaginable. The Days Inn, Howard Johnson's, and the Holiday Inn, often costing well over a hundred dollars a night, seemed like luxury hotels. Meanwhile, if Bob White's Chicken Shack Motel cost forty dollars, it would win out every time. Cheap was really the only amenity that mattered. One of the worst motels I ever stayed in was on Lake Champlain: a blatant rip-off of the Red Roof Inn. There was a horrible smell everywhere, like a liver was hanging over the door. The room sported thick orange shag carpet that hadn't been shampooed since 1982. The air conditioner was busted. And, just like it was in 90 percent of these holes, the TV screen was green! Have fun watching that! I'd have been better off in a crack house than in that motel. At least with all the lighters getting sparked, crack houses have heat.

These places were sketchier than crack houses, too. Up on Lake Hopatcong, I stopped at a Bates Motel look-alike. I walked into the "office," which was a glorified term for the owner's bedroom. "Hello!" No answer. So I walked outside . . . and I'll never forget the horrid scene waiting for me. A gravelly, old-lady voice yelled, "Hey! Hey! I'll be right there!" I looked up, and this old woman, maybe sixty-five, is hanging out the window and she has no top on! I'm not lying! Her saggy, *Evil Dead* titties were hanging down, dude! I just got in the truck and left. She could have charged me for an entire week and I wouldn't have cared! But when you can't afford to be picky, you end up at the Topless Old Lady Motel. Anglers aren't looking for a hot tub or cable TV, just a space to park the truck and an electric hookup to charge your boat batteries.

Hot Electricity

Occasionally, the room was eliminated altogether. Sometimes, during a fifteen-hour drive, I'd stop after ten hours to take a break, but I wasn't about to pay for a hotel just to get a few hours of sleep. If my batteries were charged, I'd sleep in a rest stop. But it was really common for Invitationals to butt up against Red Mans, so as I went from one event to another, I had to charge my batteries along the way. I'd roll through towns, looking for parking lots to swipe electricity. I can't tell you how many times I sucked up power from ACME, CVS, or the Dollar General.

The key was stealth. You don't head straight to the Coke machine with a bright orange cable. I'd strategically run the cord through a bush so nobody saw it, and sleep in the truck while charging up. Sometimes it was so cold, I'd bundle up under a sleeping bag and extra blanket, but still wake up shivering. The police were usually cool if they caught me. Half of them are weekend fishermen themselves, so at least they were always polite when they ran me off.

Life with the Ugly Clan

Early on in the Red Man and Federation days, I traveled with buddies I made on the tours—Pete Gluszek, Jeff Hippert, Marcel Veenstra, Dave Mansue, Mark Schafer, Bob Soley, and Tim Roach. That was the original Ugly Clan! We all became close on the Red Man and Federation circuits, so we decided to start rooming together as time went on. All eight of us were dead broke, so traveling as this big unit saved money, provided a little piece of mind, and a large sense of family. That made life on the road a lot nicer.

Trashy Living

One of the first times the Ugly Clan stayed together was in 1997 during the New York Invitational, right outside of Clayton, New York, by the Saint Lawrence Seaway. It was me, Hippert, Veenstra, Gluszek, Mansue, Schafer, and Soley, all mashed in a cabin designed to sleep four. It was just like a frat house, a constant, nonstop carnival of ball busting. Right away, the trash can in the kitchen started filling up. As the days went by, people kept piling trash on top, but nobody emptied it. By the middle of the week, the pile just stank of rotten food and garbage. By the time we had to check out, the trash was about five feet high. Nobody wanted to do anything with it. We had to draw straws to see who'd clean it up. Gluszek

HIDDEN GEMS ON TOUR

So you've just read about all the terrifying places anglers sometimes end up on the road. But don't worry. Not everywhere
sucks. Along the trail we get to some great hidden gems that
may make life on the road more enjoyable. Here are some of my
favorites.

1. *Lake Champlain, Burlington, VT.* Downtown
Burlington, a classic college town with Ben and Jerry's, the
Vermont Teddy Bear Company, and tons of bars. What else can
you ask for?

2. *Louisiana Delta, New Orleans, LA.* Bourbon Street,
a world-famous party destination where I got to celebrate my
Classic win in style. Smith and Wollensky for dinner and
Hurricanes all night for dessert!

3. *Lake Seminole, Banbridge, GA.* Wingate's Lodge, a
famous place to launch your boat, get a great home-cooked
southern meal, and hear and tell some amazing fish stories.

4. *Lake Dardanelle, Russellville, AR.* The North Forty
Bar, sitting in the middle of nowhere, is a perfect place to hear a
strange mix of country music and hip-hop, drink an ice-cold
beer, and see a few fine ladies.

5. *Cossa River Chain, AL.* This is the only place in the
country where every night is college night. With 4 Points in
Birmingham and T-Town, fun is just an hour's drive from several
world-class spotted bass lakes.

6. *Lake Ricobayo, Valladolid, Spain.* **Site of an international bass competition called the Europe Cup. Amazing food, world-class wine, and no ugly women. Wow, I wish every place we went was this good!**

lost and got stuck cleaning up that monstrosity. Drawing straws or flipping coins became our method for sticking someone with the crappy jobs. We did it all the time. One thing everyone hated to do was drive their own truck to angler meetings, because we had all claimed parking spots and outlets to juice our batteries, and nobody wanted to give up theirs. That's when it started. "I ain't driving! I ain't unhooking!" So we'd flip or draw straws to see who'd have to drive. Those short straws screwed a lot of dudes and their boat batteries.

GOOD . . . AND GOOD FOR YOU

The guys, especially Mansue, would always make a big production every night for dinner. Screw that. I didn't want to lose research time just to sit down for an elaborate meal, and besides that, I was usually the last one off the water anyway. By the time I got home, everything would be cold. So I lived off microwave pizza, chicken fingers, or other fast food. I love that stuff! Mansue would always bust my chops over it, too. "Mike's impossible to cook for unless you can cook Arby's." I'd go to the local grocery store and buy microwavable anything. Then I'd throw it in "The Cooler," a little box I had that could keep food hot or cold depending on how I turned the dial, and live off that for a week. Or I'd stock up on fast food. Sometimes, these boonie tournament towns didn't even have the Golden Arches, so I'd hit the last McDonald's outside of boonie-ville, order twelve cheeseburgers and ten boxes of nuggets, and just reheat the stuff all week. I'd be scarfing shriveled-up McDonald's on Friday that I'd bought on Tuesday. Even the Ugly Clan was appalled. But I liked it and it saved me time. My blood pressure and cholesterol are probably trashed, though. I've never had them checked, but I imagine I did enough damage that I'll probably drop dead in about five years.

THE WORLD'S GREATEST ROOMMATE

Because theft at these horrible motels can be a problem, when I'm on the road, I take most of my rods and my main tackle bag into my room every night. As a result, my equipment has a tendency to take up the whole room. My roommates would always complain that I left them with only two square feet of their own. Sometimes I'd sleep with tackle and stuff in my bed. I'm a sick freak, I know. But Pete's only slightly better than me. I'll never forget in 2002, at Lake Guntersville, when he and I stayed in a motel called Crescent Cove, a typical low-rent palace. The night before a tournament, we were spooling rods, sorting our tackle, and getting our gear together, so our stuff was everywhere. As Soley used to say about any room I stayed in, it looked like a bomb went off in a sporting goods store. We had our door open, and when Larry Nixon walked past, he literally did a double take, totally bug-eyed. I can only imagine how ridiculous he thought we were as he just shook his head and kept on walking.

But clutter was only the tip of the "Why Not to Room with Ike" iceberg. The worst thing in the world an angler can do is oversleep, so to keep that from happening, I've developed a super security system. No matter where I'm staying, from the worst dive to the top-notch hotels I'll stay in for the Classic, it never changes. The system starts with a windup alarm clock and a plug-in clock radio, which I use in addition to the one provided by the hotel. Then, after I've set those three alarms, I'll put in a wake-up call on top of everything. It's foolproof. If the electricity goes out, I've got the windup. If the windup breaks, the wake-up call rings. But the Ugly Clan used to hate me, because the whole process creates a horrible racket before the crack of dawn. I stagger each alarm about five minutes apart, so smashing one clock doesn't do any good. Anyone rooming with me is getting up when I do, like it or not. So I take up tons of space in the room, *and* I'm loud. But if anyone needs a room-mate for a fishing trip, I'm game!

Buggs Island '97, with Kevin VanDam

Fishing is a lot like golf, in that the same guys don't win every week. A guy who finishes in the Top 20 week in and week out will be one of the most solid dudes on tour. By '97, even though I wasn't winning a lot, I was starting to see more of those solid results. One of my best came at the '97 Virginia Invitational at Buggs Island, one of the first Invitationals I'd ever fished (now they're called Opens, basically semi-pro events). But while the finish was memorable, it was my second day, fishing with Kevin VanDam, that really sticks out in my memory. I hadn't really seen him since that day in '94 when we locked eyes as I sat in the boat I'd just won on Lake Norman. That look said "We'll meet again," and boy, was he right. When we launched, I was in the hunt, but Kevin was in first place. Plus, he was a pro, and I was an amateur, so etiquette meant we would work off his plan for the day, not mine. But I knew I had a shot at winning, so I wasn't going to sit like a scared little boy on the back of the boat. I let him know my spot was only ten miles away, in case his wasn't working out. Then, and this was pretty bold, I asked if he minded if both of us fished off the front deck. If I had been in fiftieth place, I'd have stayed in back and caught whatever I could, but I was sitting in the Top 5 and wanted an equal opportunity to get to the quality cover. Kevin would still get better front positioning, and ultimately would have control. But even fishing in a secondary position off the front would give me way better angles than sitting back in the dust. I think he was a little surprised I asked, but he was cool with it.

We hit his water and he caught the first fish, a little keeper. Then I caught a good one right behind him. For a good three hours, we were toe to toe. Dave Mansue had told me once that Kevin VanDam is the only guy he'd seen that might fish faster than me, so the two of us on the same boat meant the fishing was going at a wild pace. It was an amazing scenario. This was only my second year fishing Invitationals, I was paired with one of the best anglers in the world, and I was holding my own. As much as I was impressed with Kevin, I was there to win, too. The pressure just kept building and building, and I'll never forget what came next. Kevin looked back at me and yelled, "Can't you cut me a break! I'm winning this tournament. You're gonna be winning a tournament one day, and I'm gonna do this to you!"

I was blown away. I didn't think I was stepping on Kevin's toes. We had talked about the setup that morning before we even got going, and I told him that. But very calmly I jumped in the back and fished there the rest of the day. We both quietly caught our limits, but inside, I was upset and angry. I'd seen Denny intimidate Tommy Biffle back on Lake Norman in '92, but this was one of the first times I had personally seen how important intimidation can be in tournaments. I realized, later, that he was trying to get me to lay off, to not fish as hard. But at the time, my feelings were kind of hurt. It sounds stupid, I know, but here's this dude that I respected and then he pulls this? And at the end of the day, he accomplished his goal of staying in first. I stayed in the Top 5, so I had a great day too. But could it have been better? Maybe. Another valuable lesson learned.

I left the water upset and hurt, but here's the cool part. Kevin and I had met at a ramp a couple of miles from where we launched. So after the weigh-in, I had to ride with him in the boat to get back to my truck, which was across the lake. I didn't even want to sit next to the guy. Then, as we were riding, he apologized. "Mike, I'm sorry. I was just getting frustrated. I gotta be honest, you really remind me a lot of me when I was at your level." How cool is that! Kevin's only about four or five years older, but he broke into the top levels of our sport way earlier than I did. Hearing those words from him meant a lot, and taught me that what happens on the water is about winning, not about getting personal. By the time we got to my truck, it was all cleared up. Later, when I told

Ed Nailor and some other buddies about what happened, they were like "Screw Kevin VanDam!" And I said, "No, no. He's a good guy." It's always great to fish with someone you respect, and it turns out he's cool to boot.

King Hopatcong

In 1998 I started settling into who I am as a fisherman. When I was out on the water, I felt totally comfortable with the decisions I was making in research, practice, and competition. I began to close out events, turning those Top 10's and Top 5's into victories. That's not easy to do. There are guys who have fished on tour for fifteen years who have never won. I took my first Federation tournament and my first Red Man, but my best tournament of the year, the one where I really showed my potential, came during a single-day Federation tournament on Lake Hopatcong in New Jersey. Going into the tournament, I felt like I was at a disadvantage, because even though I knew the lake, Hopatcong is *the* lake for Jersey anglers. That meant I'd be facing guys who fished there week in and week out. I was determined not to let that bother me.

I turned Lake Hopatcong upside down, capturing 19.58 pounds, a lake record, as well as a one-day Federation tournament record. That felt incredible. Most Federation guys fished the lake almost daily, and had a huge leg up on me. But none of them shattered the old record of 18.06 pounds!

I started the day grass fishing, and pulled out a couple of nice keepers, both between two and three pounds. Once the sun was up and the boat traffic got heavy, I hit the docks, where I was slipping a Stone Jig in between six-inch cracks. I was drilling insanely tight targets, and the results were awesome! Boom! Four pounds! Fifteen minutes later, a five-pounder! Half an hour later, another five-pounder! Talk about getting into the zone, man! By the time it was over, I had pulled that record weight of 19.58 pounds. I'd caught that kind of weight only a handful of times, and only during fun fishing or in practice. To do it in a tournament was amazing.

Even better, I had picked the right tournament to blow up. I was paired that day with a press observer from the *Newark Star-Ledger*. For New Jersey, that's a pretty big paper, and it would give me exposure I knew would be good. Sponsors definitely read it. I was aware of that, so while I didn't quite "go Ike," this was the first tournament I allowed myself to display some natural emotion, cheering and yelling throughout the day. But even that smaller display was pushing it, in the eyes of some of my competitors. I was already an outsider, with long hair at the time, a tattoo on my shoulder, and people were like, "Who is this dude?" Established fishermen, with the exception of guys like Marcel Veenstra, Ed "Woody" Woodward, and Timmy Roach, were still standoffish. But at least nobody told me off to my face. Well, not yet, at least. But that's another story.

13 HOW I FIT IN . . . SORT OF

BASS's Daddy—Ray Scott

One fateful day in 1967, Ray Scott managed to get 106 anglers together at Beaver Lake in Arkansas for the first All-American Invitational tournament. One year later, BASS was born. Ray made a reality out of the concept of professional bass fishing and bass fishing clubs across the country. There was nothing like it before he came along, pushing his vision. People must have said, "What are you thinking, Ray? This is nonsense." But he talked people into investing, got that first tournament up and running, and people were just amazed at the results. The growth of tournament bass can be traced directly to Ray. Even our "catch and release" ethic adopted by nearly every bass fisherman on the planet can be traced to Ray. In 1972, BASS launched their "Don't Kill Your Catch" campaign to help preserve bass populations and respect the environment, not just in the places we fish, but in all recreational fisheries.

Even cooler were the technologies that came out of "catch and release," like aerator systems and additives we put in our live wells to help keep the fish alive until they're released.

Then, in 1986, he sold his shares to Helen Sevier. To say we missed him badly would be an understatement. In 2004, ESPN brought him back to help with membership drives and serve as an "amBASSador" for the sport. Great move. Ray is a smooth salesman, a charmer who makes you feel like you've known him for ten years the first time he shakes your hand. And above all, even after all these years, he's an innovator. And that's what our sport really needs.

I use Ray as a model, in the sense that I'm trying to follow in the footsteps of a guy pushing the envelope. I first met Ray in passing when he was the MC for the weigh-in at the Lake Norman tournament in 1992. To have even a few seconds with him was a thrill. But I didn't actually get to know Ray until after I won on the Louisiana Delta in '03. I sent him a letter, thanking him for starting the sport and giving me the opportunity to fish and win a Classic. He wrote back, saying, "You're doing awesome things for the sport. Keep it up." That was incredible. I still have the letter to this day, and it was the start of what, for me, is an amazing friendship.

Helen and Napoleon

Modern tournament bass fishing owes its entire identity to Ray. It wouldn't exist without him. And nothing made this more obvious than when Ray sold his shares of BASS to Helen Sevier, one of his shareholders. In my opinion, as soon as Helen took over in 1986, BASS hit a flat spot and grew stagnant until ESPN bought it in 2001. The worst thing about her regime may have been Dewey Kendrick. I think Dewey's official title was Tournament Director, but it should have been "Napoleon of BASS." He was a little dude, maybe five foot one, with a stuck-up, snot-nosed, hand-in-the-waistline attitude. It didn't make him many friends. I

heard a story about when Dewey was in Florida for a saltwater tournament event not affiliated with BASS. He was being his normal Napoleon
self, strutting around like he was some hotshot, and somehow got into it
with a saltwater angler. Dude knocked him out cold! With the media and
audience around! Man, I wish I had seen it!

I think Dewey was universally unpopular, even with a few of the good
ol' boys. But he fit into Helen's vision, which was anti-change. The organization was dedicated to the status quo, and because of that, didn't do a
lot to advance the sport. Their old-school, close-minded attitude ran
through the entire organization: "Let's just leave the sport *exactly* the
way it is." That mindset made Northern and Western anglers feel like outsiders, like everyone was against us. And when I showed up, this South
Jersey angler who went wild on the water, played loud hip-hop music, and
had tats on my body, I represented nothing but change. So I sure felt like
the old guard was against me, that's for sure.

Bitter Jim Bitter

That never felt clearer than in '99, when I fished the BASS Florida
Invitational on the St. Johns River. After two days, I was in the Top 10,
and on the last day, I locked into the Rodman Reservoir, where I had
success in practice. But this time I struggled, catching only four small
keepers. When it was time to go, I returned to the lock about ten minutes early, to make sure I didn't miss the time when it opened up to let
boats back through. There were a lot of other fishermen around too, all
waiting to do the same thing. I wasn't about to waste ten minutes of fishing time. But the fifty feet approaching the lock were marked as off-limits. No problem. I went well beyond the forbidden fifty feet, dropped my
trolling motor on high, and started pitching my Stone Jig. On my third
cast, boom! I landed an eight-pounder! Just a huge fish! All of a sudden,
I was in business. This fish would probably keep me in second or third
place, which would help give me enough points to make the tours and

the Classic, maybe even get me the Northeast Federation Angler of the Year. So I freaked, going full Ike!

That should have been the happy ending to a tough day of fishing, but it wasn't. I started the day on a stretch of bank where I had caught a couple of fish the day before, when, out of nowhere, I see this boat coming right at me, and this voice was screaming, "What are you doing? This is my stretch! I've been fishing it all day!" It was Jim Bitter, a pro I didn't really know. (He may have the most appropriate name in the world, too. Back in the '89 Classic, he dropped a keeper off the side of his boat, then went on to lose the tournament by 2 ounces! Since then, he's been mad at the world.) He totally took me by surprise. I said, "Jim, I fished here yesterday. I just pulled up on GPS!" That didn't fase him. He just kept yelling at me, basically claiming the area was his. Excuse me? We were both in contention, and had both fished that bank since the first day. All bets were off. Still, there was plenty of space for both of us. I said, "I'll go around you. What part do you want?" He stretched his arms out, indicating "all of it." This was getting ridiculous, so I decided to just let him have his way. But he was still cursing me out! I was trying . . . to . . . stay . . . calm, go around him, and start fishing again. Just as I passed him, on my second cast, boom! I caught one. That drove Jim right over the edge! He actually started casting his jerkbait at me, trying to run me off! Those things have sharp hooks. Nobody has ever done that to me. I started yelling, "Jim, relax!" but he kept casting at me! I finally said, "Look, my name is Mike Iaconelli from New Jersey. I'm staying at the Moors Inn. If you got a problem, come see me later." And he said, "I don't care where you're from. Screw you and everybody from New Jersey!"

Screw everybody in New Jersey? Everybody? Even the Unique Rockers?

I'd had enough, and just left. But the whole thing got me pretty frazzled, and I started to struggle big-time. But I made up for it back at the lock with that eight-pounder, which led to a great finish. As we were waiting for the award presentation, the tournament director said he needed to talk to me. "Mike, were you fishing by the lock at the end of the day?"

"Yeah . . ."

"Well, we had a protest filed saying you were fishing within the off-limits area."

I couldn't believe it. "No, that's not true. Ask my partner."

"Well, we're gonna give you the check right now, but don't cash it, because you're gonna have to come in for a polygraph."

What? I asked who filed the protest. "Well, we don't have the liberty to say right now, Mike." But they were at liberty to make me take a polygraph? That's sure fair. And here's the kicker. I had to go to BASS headquarters in Montgomery, Alabama, for it. Thankfully, I was going to be in the area to practice for a tournament on Lake Martin, near Montgomery. But still, it was a pain in the neck. But fine. I went down to take the polygraph. I was annoyed at the hassle, but wasn't really sweating the test, because I knew I was fishing way outside fifty feet from the lock.

That assuredness didn't make the process any more fun. I sat down with all these old-school, Southern guys staring at me the entire test, while this dude who was supposedly "licensed to do polygraphs" hooked me to the machine. Whatever. I had nothing to hide. But afterward, Napoleon Dewey said, "Mike, you failed the polygraph." I went from polite to ballistic and demanded another test. Dewey and I got into a heated discussion. They said I could take them to court, but I wasn't getting another test. What Mickey Mouse crap! No major sport would try to pull this kind of stunt with one of their athletes. Pay lawyer fees or accept it? At the time, I was just trying to make it. Even if I had the money to fight it, what would have been the end result? I probably would have been ostracized from the BASS organization. I couldn't afford that. I had to think of the big picture, so I bent over and took it.

They tried to make me feel better by saying I'd lose the day's catch, as opposed to getting disqualified entirely. Like that was supposed to make up for the lost money? I was struggling to break in, and that lost day's catch cost me at least a few grand. This was all so bushwhacked.

That was an extreme situation, but it shows why I always felt like an outsider, first from the way Jim Bitter treated me, and then the way BASS handled the protest. Their attitude was "We're Helen and Napoleon Dewey. We're the BASS organization. This is a Southern organization, so don't mess with us." I honestly got the perception that they were afraid of change, especially when it came to newer anglers coming down the pike. While I'm pretty sure neither one of them liked me, they really resented anyone who wasn't part of bass fishing's traditional makeup. We all fought the culture. "He's a Yankee. He's not really what we're looking for, anyway. So who cares how he's treated?" That's the culture I was up against, and the culture that changed when ESPN came along. That's how the old regime worked. "It's our way or get out." That would never happen today, because ESPN, BASS, and Irwin Jacobs, who heads the FLW tour, wouldn't let it happen. That's why our sport is on the verge of becoming huge.

TATTOOS

Like I said, fishing is only now starting to join us here in modern times. If I ever took off my shirt at a tournament and put all my ink on display, I'm pretty sure the shock would send a few people to the hospital. Bass fishing's hardly the NBA, where tatted-out athletes are the norm. But anyone who thinks I had them done as a stunt or some drunken accident is way off base. Ever since high school I've been intrigued by body art and how people use it to express themselves. I put the same kind of research and preparation into choosing a tattoo as I do with fishing. As a result, each of the five pieces on my body has significance and meaning to me.

THE GARGOYLE. The gargoyle on my left shoulder was my first, which I got while I was twenty-one or twenty-two. People some-times freak out when they see it, thinking I'm into black magic or sacrificing kittens. They don't realize gargoyles are protec-tors. People put stone gargoyles on buildings to protect what's inside from evil spirits and to ward off enemies. This reflected how I wanted to protect what's inside myself. I scoured the li-brary for gargoyle drawings, and found a sketch from Gothic times that I updated in black art, black ink only.

LOVE, FAITH, SPIRIT. This piece, the Chinese characters for *love, faith,* and *spirit,* runs diagonally along my left rib cage, also in black art. I had it done during my first breakup with Kristi, after I decided not to go into advertising. Its significance comes from the meaning those words have for me. Love for my family. Faith in myself, the world, and knowing things happen for a reason. The spirit to follow my quest to be a professional angler, despite any obstacles. I've always been interested in Asian culture and tradition, so using Chinese characters to ex-press myself seemed natural to me.

THE BASS. This one sits at the top of my right biceps. I wanted to commemorate my breakthrough victory as an amateur at the 1999 BASS Federation Nationals on the Red River. I searched long and hard for just the right bass picture, but even though I've got virtually every *Bassmaster* magazine ever produced, I could-n't find one that worked! Then I was going through some old boxes and found a Christmas card from a Top Rod buddy, Big John Milchinowski. It had a pic of an amazing, honkin' big bass blowing out of the water! I loved the action of that fish exploding through the surface, just like that first bass I caught in the

Poconos. The search was over. I colored this one with greens, blues, and browns to give it a true-life feel.

KEITH HARING. This was my fourth tattoo, which I got in 2001. Like the Chinese characters, this piece came out of hard times. I was doing badly on the trail during my second pro season, and my uncle Don was dealing with Hodgkin's disease. I've always loved Keith Haring's artwork, going back to middle school when I used to draw graffiti. It always represented life—the struggles you go through, the positive and negative forces that pull you in different directions. I was looking through one of my Haring books and saw an untitled series from 1985, depicting a circle with different figures inside, trying to reach a person in the center, whom I pictured as myself. I love how it's drawn on my body and am particularly proud of the colors, with different shades of black and red that really stand out.

THE HEART. The roots of this enormous piece actually go back to '98. I had gotten back together with Kristi, and we thought we'd spend our lives together. Like many devoted, and ultimately shortsighted, couples, we wanted to get something as a symbol of our commitment. About six months before we got married, I had Kristi's name written in Old English-style text across my lower back. Kristi stepped up too, inking on her back a cherub, holding a heart with my name inside. At the time, both were deeply meaningful to us. They eventually turned into examples of why you should never tattoo a person's name on your body.

But I eventually turned it into my favorite and most meaningful piece, which took several months to design and now sprawls across most of my back. It revolves around the Tree of Life, with some leaves growing, and some that are dead. They symbolize how some paths in life are successful and live on, while others wither and die. Near the bottom are the trunk and roots, representing my past and what I've been through. Inside the trunk, it says "Pain." The roots below form the word "is" out of "I" and "S" from my original "Kristi" tattoo. The rest of "Kristi" is covered, but I wanted to keep some of it, because that time in my life is still a part of me, it's just something different now. The sentence "Pain is" has no ending yet. It's a work in progress, something I'll fill in as I continue to live. Thus far, the piece has taken five sittings of four hours each, so I'm obviously willing to be patient to make sure it's perfect.

The last part is a sacred heart, which sits in front of the tree. I'd never claim to be a devout churchgoer, but the heart represents my belief in a higher spirit. It also represents my own heart and soul. Gargoyles are on each side of the heart, one of which is stabbing it with a spear, representing my heart being wounded. But like so many times in my life, my heart heals and what's left behind is beautiful. I see it as literally art reflecting life.

14 STARTING A FAMILY

Finding out Kristi's Pregnant

Right around Christmas in 1997, Kristi had a hunch she might be pregnant, and made an appointment to find out. I guess a woman knows, right? We had planned on getting married before having a baby, so things were a little out of order. (We didn't actually get married until April of 1999.) But I really wanted kids, so I can't describe how excited I was. It felt like we were finally growing up and getting out on our own. I had my job at Dick's, Kristi was supportive of my fishing goals, and our families were excited for us. Everything felt perfect, even with the extra pressure of having to make a professional fishing career work for three. I didn't want to stay at Dick's forever, and I was even more motivated to succeed.

Kristi and I did all the first-time parent stuff. We did Lamaze, which was so stupid I could barely take it. But Kristi wanted to do it, so we did (although in the end, I think even she thought it was a little stupid, too). It was all part of the drill. Everything was great. But nothing in the life of a professional fisherman stays smooth and simple for long.

Commuting for Drew

Kristi was due in early September, and I had no tournaments scheduled until October. Sweet! I was all set to be there for the birth. But when her due date rolled around, it just kept rolling on past! We waited. And waited. And waited some more. Before we knew it, the practice period for the 1998 Virginia Invitational at Buggs Island was about to begin. I really wanted to be there for the birth, but absolutely had to fish that event if I wanted a chance of making the tours next season, and there was no sign of a baby coming. It was a mess. Finally, Kristi said, "Just go. I'll probably be another week, anyway. Don't worry." I was a wreck, but with my cell phone never leaving my side, I hit the road.

The first day of practice went well. The fish were biting, and still no baby. I spent a solid second day scouting my topwater B plan. When I headed back to the ramp at about six P.M., I noticed my phone battery was dead. Uh-oh. Once I gave it some juice, it lit up with missed calls! My mom's house. Her mom's house. I dropped my boat off at the hotel and raced back to New Jersey, pushing 100 mph the whole way, not easy in a Suburban. I've never driven with such total disregard for the law. I wasn't worried about getting pulled over. I'd just tell the cop, "If you're gonna give me the ticket, give me the ticket. I gotta go!"

I got to the hospital around eleven that night, with plenty of time to spare. Drew Taylor Iaconelli, my first daughter, was born around around 4 A.M. on September 29, 1998. They let me play "catcher" and cut the cord thingee. The experience of watching my baby come into this world was amazing. I'm hard to bring to tears, but I got very emotional and was so grateful to be there for her birth.

Of course, I still had to take care of the fishing. I sat with Kristi all morning and missed the last day of practice, not that I cared. But the official registration was from three to six o'clock that afternoon. If I didn't register, I wasn't fishing, and wouldn't have a chance to turn pro. I had to go. Story of my life. I got back in the truck, stoked that Drew had arrived and upset I had to leave her. I averaged "only" 90 mph on the way back, and made the registration. My buddies handed out cigars at registration and made a big announcement. That was cool. I managed to keep my focus on the water, even though Kristi and the baby never left my thoughts. I ended up with an amazing fifth-place finish and a much-needed check for $7,000 (I had a family to feed!), but the tournament seemed kind of pointless. I wanted my trophy and cash ASAP so I could get back home to my wife and child. The fishing gods had smiled on me. I had made it for the birth, and still kicked butt in a very important tournament. It was all meant to be.

15

SHREVEPORT '99, THE FEDERATION NATIONALS

Reaching the Classic through the Federation is a long, complicated, and really difficult process. Hundreds of thousands of anglers from across the country (and even Japan and Zimbabwe) are shooting for the same goal. Only five make it, one from each region—Western, Central, Southern, Northern, and Eastern. I had beaten a team of Jersey anglers on Lake Winnipesaukee to earn the right to represent my state at the '99 Federation Nationals on the Red River outside Shreveport, Louisiana. Now I had to beat the nine other anglers from my region, made up of New York, Vermont, Connecticut, New Hampshire, Maine, Delaware, Maryland, Massachusetts, Pennsylvania, and New Jersey (me again!), to earn my Classic berth. I didn't have to beat the whole field, just those nine dudes. But I figured the only surefire way to make that happen was to win the whole tournament, so that was my approach.

The Honeymoon Not-So-Sweet

I planned to go into the tournament refreshed, and on a major high. In April of 1999, Kristi and I finally got married, ending the longest series of off-and-on dating and broken engagements in the history of America. It was a great wedding. Everyone had a blast, especially when all my high school friends and I started breakdancing. We could still do our signature moves, even after all these years! I guess we broke the Unique Rockers up too early.

Then Kristi and I went to St. Lucia for our honeymoon. Everything was going well until a storm hit on our last day there, and we were stuck. When I realized we weren't getting out that day and I'd miss a full day of pre-practice, I totally freaked out! I may not have ruined the entire honeymoon for Kristi, but I probably came close, pacing around the honeymoon suite until she threw my fidgety butt out. Then I paced around the hotel. All these Caribbean hostesses were smiling and trying to help, saying, "Hey, mon! Cheer up. You can go fishing any day, mon!" I didn't even bother trying to explain. Eventually I realized there was nothing I could do but wait. At least I'd have the best tan in Shreveport!

Marking My Territory

After a terrible first day of practice, I started to turn it around on my second and third days. But I still didn't feel like I was around the winning fish. The Red River is full of backwater, these newly formed flooded areas, with nothing but trees and even more backwater behind them. Finding a sweet spot here was worse than looking for a needle in a haystack. I had found some aerial photos of the fishery that showed a huge area of perfect-looking water behind a huge stand of trees. On Day Four, I busted my butt until it was almost dark, found some trails, and worked my way in there. I had only about half an hour to fish, but I caught four or five big ones right away. I spent my last practice day defining and expanding the area, and must have caught fifty! Sold! All that was left to do was carefully mark off my GPS points, and I'd have my winning spot.

About a month later, I was back in Shreveport for the two practice days right before the tournament. I was psyched, ready to rock and roll. But on my first day, I caught only one small one. Oh, no! But instead of panicking, I stayed calm and made adjustments on my second and last practice day. Instead of sitting in the shallows near the bank, the fish were actually suspended on the edge of the treeline. These were post-spawn fish, on a different pattern than a month before when I first found them, but I successfully redefined the area. That made me confident about my chances, which was huge, because win or lose, after the Nationals I was going pro, leaving the Federation and my last ten years as a club fisherman behind. I was ready to go out with a bang.

The Northeastern Legacy

I wanted to follow in the footsteps of Bryan Kerchal, the only angler to win the Federation Nationals and the Bassmaster Classic. He was from Connecticut, a fellow Yankee, and a guy all the northeastern anglers tried to emulate. Tragically, Bryan died in a plane crash only months after winning the '94 Classic. It was horrible. I never had a chance to meet him, but I remember getting chills after his victory on North Carolina's High Rock Lake. I was stoked for him, for the Northeast, and for the Federation. It felt like the whole area was on a roll. Then, suddenly, he was gone.

Bryan was considered the Federation's great hope. For a while after, Pete Gluszek was the guy. Despite the fact that he's had a great career, Pete didn't do it fast enough for some people. I was next in line. The similarities were there. We're all anglers from the Northeast who went from clubs to the Federation to the pros. It's just not a path most anglers take. We're few and far between. Most guys just skip the Federation level and hit the semi-pro and pro events. That's why I'm so proud to represent the Federation, and still recognize myself as a Federation angler, even though I turned pro over five years ago.

DAY ONE—BRUCE LYNCH!

Having successfully redefined my area on the last day of practice, I was stoked that first day of the tournament. I headed down to my oxbow, that little bend in the river that held my magic backwater lake. Two boats had beaten me there, but at thirty acres, there was space for three. I started swimming a Stone Jig at those fish suspended around the trees, and right away found myself in the zone. I finished with over seventeen pounds in my well, a huge sack. At the weigh-in line, people were impressed, but something felt off. I found out Bruce Lynch, representing Delaware (another state in my region), came in with nearly twenty-one pounds! I was in second place for the entire tournament, but it wouldn't mean squat if another angler in my division came in first. In any other situation, I'd have been stoked off my rocker. Here, I was four pounds in the hole. But I knew I couldn't give up. I'd just have to keep hunting and pecking.

DAY TWO—FISH THE MOMENT, IDIOT!

Day One had been windy and cloudy, but the next day was exactly the opposite. Bluebird skies, sunny, with no clouds. I was swimming my 3/8-ounce Stone Jig in exactly the same way I had slaughtered them the day before, but was seriously struggling. After three hours, I didn't have a keeper. In frustration, I threw my jig and didn't bother swimming it back. I just let it sink before beginning my retrieve. Boom! I caught my first one. Then, bling! You could practically see the lightbulb glowing over my head.

The most common sin anglers make is not fishing the moment, but trying to catch them like you did the day, week, or month before. That's exactly what I was doing, going after Day Two's fish with Day One's strategy.

The day before, the windy conditions pushed the fish high in the water column. Now that it was sunny and still, they went back down to the bottom half. I had spent the entire morning running my lure above the fish. I swapped out the 3/8-ounce jig for a 1/2-ounce in the same exact color and a trailer that would drop lower in the water. Right away, I started chunking again, but because I had lost so much time, I brought in only around thirteen pounds. Rodney Wagley, a local angler from Baton Rouge, caught almost seventeen pounds, dropping me to third, but thankfully, Bruce had a tough day too. He was still in first, but his lead over me was down to three pounds. Rodney could catch fifty pounds tomorrow for all I cared. I needed to catch Bruce. Had I just stopped to think instead of wasting the first three hours on the water, I'd have already done it.

ADJUSTING THE ATTACK

Going into the last day, a Saturday, I had a feeling there'd be more local boats on the lake, which would put tons of extra pressure on my primary pattern. So I decided to start in my backup spot about five miles downriver, which I called the "Community Hole." I hadn't fished there since pre-practice the month before, but I just had that *feeling*, like I *needed* to start the day with one hot lap there, only for an hour, and then go back to my A plan. I'd lose about an hour and a half in travel time, which could be significant, but I had to trust my gut.

Taking from the Community, Not Giving Back

When I got to the Community Hole, I started throwing a spinnerbait along a sweet stretch of bank. I hadn't thrown one all week, but knew it was a good lure choice for two reasons. First, the bank had what I call a "reverse drop." Normally, the water becomes shallower as you approach the bank. But the main body of the Community Hole was the opposite; shallow in the center, maybe 5 feet, and deeper as it approached the trees closer to the bank. It's that deep channel by the bank that I call a reverse drop. I figured that unusual bottom structure was perfect for the fish. Second, in the drop there was a lot of little lumber, which made it almost impossible to swim a jig, because it's too heavy. A spinnerbait is more effective for the tighter lanes I needed to thread.

And mad props for the spinnerbait! I snagged two right off the bat! A half hour later, the bites stopped and I had a choice. Stay or leave? That was the million-dollar question. As I was deciding, I noticed a little bend in the trees across from the drop, where I'd had a bite a month earlier. I hadn't fished it since, but the same gut feeling told me to run a jig over it real quick. I idled over, then pitched my jig over a trunk angled horizontally in the water. *Boink!* A four-pounder! I was screaming! That was my last bite in the Community Hole, and I left when my hour was up. But *that's* what I call fishing the moment.

Gotta Love Hunches

I went back to where I'd fished the previous two days. Just like I figured, it had local boats everywhere. Some were just there to watch, some were fishing, but it was a zoo. I knew the rest of the day would be tough, but I already had eight pounds in my live well. Going to the Community Hole had really paid off. I struggled through the traffic, but kept working my half-ounce jig pattern and slowly started catching them. I continued to trust my feelings and make great decisions, and ended the day with a fifteen-pound bag. I was proud of myself, but I still didn't know if it was enough.

Going to the Classic, Baby!

Just as it's done in the Classic, they weighed us in order of our predicted finish. When they pulled me to the very back, with everybody going before me, I started feeling pretty confident. Bruce had weighed in and kept his lead. Rodney stayed in second behind Bruce, but clinched his division, so he was happy. I needed over fourteen pounds to take the lead. I pulled my fish out one by one, adding a lot of drama to the scene (they don't let us do that nearly enough anymore). The crowd loved it. My heart was pounding out of my shirt as I watched the scales. Twelve, thirteen, fourteen. . . . When it finally stopped at over fifteen pounds, I knew I had won, and was going to the Classic! Not surprisingly, I had a little freak-out, lifting the trophy up over my head and screaming, "YEAAHHH!" People looked at me like, "Whatever, spaz."

SPINNERBAITS

Another great power-fishing bait, and incredibly versatile. Spinnerbaits—safety pin-style lures with a skirt and spinning blades attached—are fantastic for covering large amounts of water. They rip through cover, getting the reaction strike that's a foundation of power fishing. Like all lures, spinnerbait savvy starts with "matching the hatch," choosing a spinnerbait that mimics what the bass are eating. Shad? Grab a spinnerbait with a white skirt. Bluegill? Use a skirt with some chartreuse and green. Yellow perch? Fire tiger skirt. I carry about a half dozen spinnerbait bodies in every size, but the blades—Colorado, Indiana or willow, colored gold, silver, copper, and everything else in the rainbow—are the key. Here's how I break them down.

WILLOW BLADE. In clear water conditions, bass often use sight as their primary sense. I want a blade with lots of flash to grab their attention, which makes a willow blade perfect. They run beautifully in deeper, crystal-clear water, where bass often hang, and their elliptical shape is great for slicing through weeds and other cover. Add a smaller willow on a spinnerbait for more control of the lure.

COLORADO BLADE. At the opposite end of the spectrum is the rounded Colorado blade. When the water's cold and muddy and the bass are huddled up at the bottom, I need a blade that creates lots of vibration, because the fish are keying in more on what they feel than see. A Colorado blade is great because its round size maximizes the amount of water displaced, which creates that great vibration I want. With a Colorado blade, I can feel the lure as it moves over the ground. I want a lure that shakes the rod out of my hand.

INDIANA BLADE. For those situations in the middle, where the water is stained and the fish are suspended around cover, I love the Indiana blade. They're longer than the Colorado, producing more flash, but their shape still allows for more vibration than a willow. Great in open water and cover, it's the perfect happy-medium blade, possibly the best all-around one in the biz.

When you get comfortable with each blade style, try combining them on your spinnerbait. Use a Colorado *and* a willow to gain some flash while keeping your vibration. Get creative and aggressive with your blade and skirt configurations. Don't assume a spinnerbait setup won't work because your buddy calls you a dummy. Give it a try and prove him wrong (or buy the beer afterward).

16

PROFESSOR IACONELLI AT YOUR SERVICE

Research 101

I had qualified to fish my first Bassmaster Classic, on the Louisiana Delta, in 1999. Technically, I was still an amateur, which would seem like a huge disadvantage. Fortunately, I had qualified through the Federation Nationals, which is basically a mini-Classic. Same format, same pressure, so I knew what to expect. For the Classic, anglers get a week of pre-fishing on the Delta up to a month before the tournament. Then, the week of the tournament, we get a single day to hit the water. In between, that fishery is off-limits. But even though I was comfortable with the format, and thought I could handle the pressure, I'd never fished the Delta, a massive fishery of approximately 500,000 acres. You launch your boat, look around, and think, "Where do I start?" That's where the extensive research I always stress comes in. I had qualified nearly two months before the official pre-practice period in late June, so right away I started my research, which is broken into two parts: off-water and on-water.

Off-water research includes everything that can be done at home in the weeks before a tournament to turn huge acres into a more manageable size. For the Delta, that meant turning 500,000 acres into 10,000. Breaking down a fishery, especially one that big, requires information. Here's how I get it.

PART ONE: HISTORICAL RESEARCH

For the '99 Classic, I rifled through old issues of *Bassmaster, Bassin'*, *BASS Times,* and every other periodical I owned, looking for articles on the Louisiana Delta, keying in on news, tournament results, and tournament write-ups. From there, I broadened my research, looking for information on tidal marsh fishing, hot weather fishing (the Delta in summer is like a sauna), and other relevant topics, making notes and looking for buzzwords that repeatedly turned up. Clues about baits, areas, vegetation, and seasonal patterns. The whole works. Soon, my notebook was filled with useful information. And that's just the start.

I hopped on the Internet to find more articles and information than I had around the house. I also contacted the Louisiana Department of Wildlife and Fisheries for studies taken after areas of the Delta are shocked, a process where electricity is pumped into the water, dazing the fish long enough to get an accurate count of species populations. This is done for fishery management, not so a bunch of anglers can get the inside dirt, but the information is really useful in showing where the fish are, and how many are there. Don't be afraid to dig beyond the seemingly obvious sources.

PART TWO: MAP STUDY

This is big. I don't want to waste time wandering around lost, especially on a huge, complicated fishery like the Delta, so I break everything down on a map ahead of time. And I use multiple map sources. Too many guys rely on just one. If ten maps of a fishery exist, I want all ten. Libraries can be a great source for maps. And again, think outside the box. In '99, I used the Internet to find a company that had taken aerial photos of the Delta, and got copies. Now, along with the two conventional maps I'd found, I had aerials, which became invaluable. My research stressed clear water would be money. On a standard map, water clarity isn't marked. But on aerial photos, clear water looks black while muddy water is lighter. Right away I was able to eliminate huge stretches of water, and find some great ones. Extra information is gold.

PART THREE: UNIVERSAL GENERAL SEASONAL OUTLINE

Once you have your maps laid out with all your pages of notes, create what I call "The Universal General Seasonal Outline." This traces the basic seasonal movements that all bass go through on any body of water, no matter if it's in Jersey, California, or even Europe. My patterns may be a little different than Takahiro Omori's, and his might be a little different than Kevin VanDam's, but they're all basically the same. Fish winter in the deepest, most vertical breaks of the lake and go shallow in the spring for spawning. In the summer, they look for deeper water, and thicker cover or current. In the fall, they again go shallow, following the bait, to fatten up for winter, and then in late fall they turn back toward their wintering areas. My seasonal pattern outline is modeled after the one Rick Clunn laid out in a three-part series of articles for *Bassmaster* magazine in 1988. All the theories and ideas about bass movements he wrote about were so dead-on, it was scary. I combined his ideas with my own experiences and ideas, and by '99 I had defined my own seasonal pattern. Now it's my bible.

On-Water Research—Electronics and Transmission Baits

The second half of a winning pretournament strategy is on-water research. The average fisherman fishes the spot he found off-water or

LOCATING BASS, PART I: SEASONAL PATTERNS

For me, locating bass comes down to the mental side of fishing, where every angler can excel. The first part involves understanding their very predictable patterns of seasonal behavior, a blueprint that holds true whether you're in New Jersey, California, Tennessee, Europe, or South America. I group them into the four seasons: winter, spring (broken into pre-spawn, spawn, and post-spawn), summer, and fall (broken into early fall and fall transition).

WINTER. In winter, the bass are lethargic and seek the warmest water—usually down deep—looking for easy access to food. So I'm looking for them in the deepest, most vertical break areas in the lake. Places where the channel swings against the bank, creating depth, or structure drops in the open-water areas.

SPRING. This season can be broken into three sections: pre-spawn, spawn, and post-spawn. You'll need to understand the differences to take full advantage of this seasonal pattern. In pre-spawn, the fish start moving out of their deep wintering grounds to areas where they stage before migrating to spawning areas. Look for isolated bits of cover on the way to spawning flats, or main lake points where they can feed. They will stop first on main points, followed by secondary points, on the way to the shallow spawning grounds. Come spawning time, warmer water is the key. I'm looking for large flats, protected coves and pockets, and hard bottom areas that are suitable for bass to spawn. During post-spawn, bass move off their beds and back toward where they staged during pre-spawn, but with a couple of differences. Mating is tough work, so they're going to be more lethargic. They'll tend to suspend, or bury themselves deeper in cover than during pre-spawn, so you may have to dig a little deeper to find them.

SUMMER. I beat three things into my brain: Deeper . . . Thicker . . . Current. Deeper, because in open areas bass will seek cooler, more oxygenated water with plenty of food flowing by. Thicker, meaning if there's heavy enough cover, they'll stay shallow even in the summer heat. I'll rip through the weeds, brush, and pads where bass are looking for shade, oxygen, and food. Current is a huge summer pattern, so look along feeder streams, headwaters, tidal bodies, or the main river. Anywhere with strong current.

FALL. Broken into early fall and fall transition. In early fall, bass know winter is coming, so they're trying to fatten up. It's feeding frenzy time, so I become very bait oriented, trying to match the hatch. I hit creeks and pockets with drains, or any fresh influx of water because they tend to attract more baitfish. Fall transition has the fish moving toward their wintering areas, so head back to those vertical breaks. Lots of times, they'll stop on isolated points or cover. Bass tend to school during fall transition, so sometimes you'll hit the jackpot off one point or single piece of cover.

while tooling around the water, but doesn't define it. That's a serious mistake. Every area where I've ever won a tournament has what I call a "sweet spot." The hot spot within the area you've targeted. The spot that wins tournaments. I start defining an area by idling in a zigzag pattern, using my electronics to find anything out of the ordinary, like sudden changes in depth or the presence of baitfish. As soon as something catches my eye, I drop a marker buoy, shut off my outboard, and drop my trolling motor. Then I break out my transmission lures to define the area further. I usually accomplish that with transmission lures like crankbaits, Carolina rigs, and heavy jigs. They help me feel what's on the bottom, revealing isolated cover like stumps, grass, or rocks that often turn into sweet spots because they hold large concentrations of fish. Most guys who are great at using transmission lures and electronics are natural deepwater fishermen. Two of the best at using electronics are Aaron Martens and Brett Hite, both West Coast guys. Because their native waters are so deep, they're experts at deciphering what's on the bottom, because they can't see it. A guy like Larry Nixon becomes an expert at defining because of his incredible instincts. He uses lures to map out the bottom like a blind man uses his hands to see. (It probably comes from his years as a guide down in Texas. When people are paying you to find fish, you turn into Sherlock Holmes real quick. The pressure is actually very similar to tournament fishing.)

After dropping your buoys and using your transmission baits to find your sweet spot, there's one more step left to on-water research. Obviously, you'll use GPS to mark the location, but don't forget to keep notes of water temperature, air temperature, wind speed, depth, bottom composition, or anything else that seems important about your sweet spot. When you get home, put that information in a master log. I never take mine out on the water, because I'm too scared of losing it. In the end, this intensive process will reward you with killer sweet spots. Unless that lake gets drained or you lose your master logbook, the information's yours forever.

Combine all those steps and you'll see the results on the water. It sounds tough, but it becomes second nature after a little while. And the positive results will motivate you to keep it up. I've been at it for so long, research no longer feels like extra work. It's all just part of the tournament process, something I take a lot of pride in doing well.

ELECTRONICS

The average angler doesn't understand how to use electronics properly, mostly because of their nickname—"fish finders." That may be the most misleading term in fishing. Why? Because electronics should be used primarily to find structure breaks and environmental change rather than to locate actual fish.

Electronics are your underwater eyes to see what the fishery's bottom looks like. Change is the key. I'm looking for anything out of the ordinary: humps, drops, channel swings, points, and isolated spots of cover. If I'm rolling across a static two-mile flat that's eight feet deep, I'm watching my depth finder for spots that suddenly drop to ten or eleven feet, then pop back to eight. That's a change in structure and contour. Then I'll float a buoy to mark the spot before fishing some transmission lures like crankbaits, Carolina rigs, and heavy jigs to better define it.

Even when I am using electronics to find fish, I'm not necessarily looking for bass. I want to see fish activity, particularly baitfish, which resemble pods or clouds on depth finders. If the water is twenty-five feet deep and the bait's at twelve, that indicates a fish activity level of twelve feet, so I'll rig my equipment for that depth. Only occasionally am I looking for that classic crescent-moon shape, the telltale sign of a game fish.

It's so important not to get caught up in that "fish finder" mentality where equipment becomes a crutch. By using your electronics to provide blueprints of structure breaks, contour changes, and groupings of baitfish, you won't have to actually see the bass to hook them.

17 THE '99 CLASSIC

t Practice

Through research, I was able to shrink the Delta's half-million acres and focus on two areas, Bayou Black and Des Almonds, each a more manageable ten thousand acres. I planned to spend three days of my pre-practice period in each, but my gut told me that Bayou Black, an inland fishery, would be better than Des Almonds. Practice confirmed my hunch. The first three days of practice in Bayou Black yielded two decent days and one really good day. But Day Four, my first in Des Almonds, was terrible. Instead of wasting two more days there, I headed back to Bayou Black to define the area, paying extra attention to spots I discovered on my most successful day. In the end, I felt confident that Bayou Black was indeed the real deal.

*N*ot Catching Anything

During my mediocre first day of practice in Bayou Black, I probably hit thirty canals with the key elements I was looking for: clear water, vegetation, and current. I only actually caught anything in only one or two canals, but that didn't discourage me, since I learn as much from not catching them as I do when I haul in a twenty-pound sack. If there are 350 canals in an area, I want to know which five are the best and eliminate the rest, taking huge areas of the map out of play and removing a lot of guesswork. Besides, catching them everywhere can mess with you, too. When the tournament comes, you're pulled in every direction and can't settle on a pattern. Those periods where I strike out are important for forming my game plan. Embracing and learning from an empty well during practice can help fill it when the tournament comes around.

On my final practice day, as I was exploring an area toward the main channel of Bayou Black called Orange Grove, the strangest thing happened. I was fishing a little canal system, when out of nowhere the current started rushing through. Current is like a dinner bell for fish, because it literally washes food past their faces. Instead of having to chase it, they sit there and chomp. Wasting no time, I threw my jig into the current and *boom!* I caught one. But in the minute it took to let the fish go, the current stopped. Two seconds later, it rushed back in, followed by a loud, very unnatural noise. This was getting bizarre. I stood on my outboard, peered out to the main canal, and noticed a tugboat going past. A lightbulb went off in my brain. When the tug passed, the water displacement created brief moments of current. There was another element I defined and tucked into my head. If I heard a tug go past, I could find the current it generated and cast into it during that tiny interval.

THE FIRST-DAY JITTERS

I'd dreamed about this day since I read my first *Bassmaster* magazine and watched guys like Rick Clunn hoist the trophy on *The Bassmasters*.

The night before the tournament started, I slept a little less, and woke up a little earlier. But even though I was somewhat awed by the whole scene, I'd been working forever to get there, and I wasn't going to let jitters get in the way. I wasn't just out to avoid embarrassing myself, either. I wanted to win, and figured it would take about fifteen pounds a day to do it. Who cares if nobody had ever won a Classic as a rookie? Someone had to be the first.

A GOOD START

Every angler gets assigned an observer to ride along in their boat, usually a camera guy or someone from the media. I have no idea why, but the first day I was assigned James Gorman from *The New York Times.* All the superstars of the sport were there. Why bother teaming a guy from a huge mainstream publication with me? I didn't understand it, but I had too much on my mind to give it much thought. As my number was called, I threw down the throttle, and officially started my first day in the Bassmaster Classic.

I decided to start Day One in a canal near Orange Grove that had some good fish, but would attract a lot of attention from other anglers. I wanted to hit it before it got too beat up. Forty minutes later, I didn't have a keeper. This was an ominous start. First day of my first Classic, in a place I thought was good for a quick catch, and I didn't get anything. So I took off for the Orange Grove. When I arrived, I dropped my trolling motor along a stretch where I had caught them pretty good a month earlier during practice. I saw beautiful wind-blown current at a sharp right-hand bend on the bank. My eyes bugged out of my face as I told James, "We're gonna catch them here." The swami was right. I started plucking them out, catching two limits, probably twelve or thirteen keepers. I was culling my butt off, and really thought I had a good shot at my fifteen-pound daily target.

Since there were no other competitors around, I was free to freak out, which is exactly what I did. I was pumping my fist, yelling and screaming as I pulled those babies from the water. My buddy from the *Times* had never covered a tournament before, and he was getting psyched right along with me. He probably thought everyone behaved like I did when they caught 'em. But I wasn't surprised I did well with the *Times* on board. For some reason, when I'm being watched, I fish better. While lots of anglers say it makes them nervous, an audience puts me in the zone. It's a chance to show my stuff and prove myself. My whole life, I've been a natural showman, be it in fishing or breakin'. I must have made an impression on Mr. Gorman, because months later, when his article came out in *The New York Times Magazine*, he used phrases like "fast talking," "fist pumping," and "excited" to describe me on the water. He pegged me before anybody knew my "style."

My First Classic Weigh-in

As I sat in a dark tunnel with the gods of bass fishing, waiting to be brought into the Superdome for the weigh-in, the awe factor set in. I'd been dreaming about this moment, had watched it on TV, and now I had made it. Finally, they called me in. The lights were bright, the music was booming, and the fans were screaming. Entering the arena during the Classic never gets old. But even with all the distractions, all I wanted to know was "What do my five fish weigh?"

"Michael Iaconelli, from Runnemede, New Jersey!" boomed through the speakers as I was directed to the stage. I had a high-quality bag, and was allowed to pull my fish out individually. With each one the crowd got more excited. People love to see those dripping wet bass come out of the well, with the biggest saved for last. I weighed in at 15-1, over my pace by an ounce, and finishing the day in fourth place, a little over a pound and a half off the lead. I was stoked! They brought the Top 5 finishers onstage for a media session, which included Davy Hite and Denny Brauer . . . plus me, down on the end by myself. It was surreal, but I handled it pretty well, until my "rookie Ike" mouth got me in trouble. I was asked if I was intimidated being in the Top 5 with so many great anglers. I looked straight at the reporter and said, "These are my heroes. I've been reading about them forever. But I'm not really competing against them. I'm competing against the fish, so I'm not really worried about these guys." *I'm not really worried about these guys?* Was I smoking crack? Everyone, media and anglers included, was staring at me, not amused. All I meant was that I see my opponent as the fish, not the anglers. I can't control what other guys do. I guess I didn't make that clear. Luckily, I didn't get a lot of questions after that, but I'll never forget how I botched that interview.

DAY TWO

After my success on Day One, I was more relaxed when I woke up for Day Two. My plan was to hit the Orange Grove again and scope out where the wind was blowing, since that's what was driving the fish to bite. I took the same two-hour drive out to that sharp right-hand bend along the bank, and dropped my trolling motor. No current. I kept fishing. Forty minutes went past. No current. I went back to my starting point from Day One. No current. Now I was really starting to worry. I licked my finger and held it up, begging for a sign of wind. Nothing! At that point, it hit me.

I'm in serious trouble.

I drove randomly around the Orange Grove, looking for canals with current. Nada. Two hours had passed, two were left, and I had no fish in my well. Then the lightbulb popped again! *"Tugboat!"* I focused on canals close to the main shipping channel, waiting for a tug to pass. The current would suck in, then out, and *boom!* I'd catch one! It was a slow and difficult pattern to time because I had no control over when a tug would cruise down a canal. I had to wait until I saw or heard something, then rush toward it. I managed to cobble together seven keepers for a limit around eleven pounds, but that was off my fifteen-pound target. I cursed myself for wasting the first two hours in an area with no current. But that was nothing compared to the cursing I did later.

My Weigh-in Protest

The tournament director at that time was a guy named Jeff Owens, who worked under "Napoleon" Kendrick. I had a decent bag, I was in fourth place, and I was representing the Federation. But Jeff looked at my fish and told me to just go bag them, instead of letting me pull them out one by one. Basically, he was giving me the brush-off. I felt wronged, whether it was purposely directed at me or not. I sat there thinking, "This is *my* dream, *my* moment!" And when I pulled up to the stage, I could see they were expecting me to grab my bag, weigh, and leave. My bag was on one side of the live well, but I kept my two big fish on the other. I took out the bag, but instead of going straight up to weigh, I put the bag on the floor and held my two big fish up for display. The crowd loved it, but I could see Napoleon with his arms crossed, burning a hole through me with his eyes. I brought home a decent 11-5, but it wasn't close to enough. Davy Hite had brought home a ridiculous 19-3 and blew everyone away. I dropped to eighth.

I headed back to the boatyard, trying to psyche myself up for a Hail Mary final day, when I got ambushed by Jeff Owens, who was screaming at me about showing off my fish. "Mike, why did you do that? I gave you strict orders to bag your fish!" I started cursing him out, laying into him about this being our chance to shine in front of fans and sponsors. He tried pushing it off on Napoleon, saying that it was his decision. I wasn't having it. "Screw that! Just for that, I'm gonna come home tomorrow with a twenty-pound bag." They'd *have* to let me show that off. It felt like the powers to be were out to get me. The only way I could get them back would be with a huge third day.

SCROUNGING TO GET BY

Big talk aside, sitting almost ten pounds behind Davy, which was a massive deficit in fishing, I really did need about twenty pounds to have a prayer of winning, and have everyone ahead of me do worse so I could gain ground. I went right back to my key areas of the Orange Grove, but there was no current in any of them. I hit a nice, isolated spot I'd tried on Day One. Nothing. Two hours were gone, and I was getting depressed. Then all of a sudden, the trees started swaying. The wind had picked up. I literally started screaming with joy! Sure as anything, a trickle of current was rolling, and I started ripping them! Unfortunately, time wasn't on my side. With about ten minutes left, I was rushing around trying to scrape up a little more weight. I pitched my jig into a little current break and hooked a good one. I felt the hook set, and *snap!* The line broke. In my rush, I'd broken a cardinal rule of fishing, and forgotten to check my line. Nobody should ever break a fish off using a seventeen-pound line, especially when you're trying to make a monumental comeback to win a Classic. That's just careless. It soured my mood heading back to the weigh-in, but at least I had salvaged the day.

Day Three Weigh-in

At the weigh-in, they staged me eighth to last, which I took as a sign that I must have had a reasonably good day. And this time, they let me lift up every fish and promote my sponsors, as I was wearing their names on my clothing. Nobody gave me any lip. Even though I didn't catch my twenty pounds, I still felt like I made my point, that I was a quality angler and deserved some respect. So I weighed in at 13-9, only enough to get second place for the moment behind Ron Shuffield. There went my dream of winning. Davy brought home another twenty pounds on his way to victory, while I finished sixth. Even if I'd landed that last fish, it would have bumped me to only second or third, tops. I took home a check for six thousand dollars, which on top of the fifteen thousand dollars I had just won at the Federation Nationals showed I was moving up in the world.

The fans reacted positively, not because I finished sixth, but because they respected how strongly I represented the Federation. Rick Clunn took the time to shake my hand and say, "Mike, hell of a job this week." Rick Clunn was congratulating me! That blew me away. Kevin VanDam also had some nice words, which was cool, because we hadn't talked since the argument we had in Virginia back in '97. I saw it as a sign that at least he respected me. My sponsors, in the meantime, were just shocked. I don't know this for sure, but I think some wrote off my success as a lucky streak. That's the vibe I got. Then again, I still feel that way to this day. Maybe it's self-created paranoia, to stay sharp and hungry. It's definitely not anything I do consciously, because I don't take the time to put myself in that mind-set. Either way, having that chip on my shoulder is a positive for me. I think that's true of a lot of athletes.

Still, after those two really huge tournaments, some of the companies that were on the fence about me came around. Dick's was one. Then came my rod and reel sponsor, Team Daiwa. (Interestingly, I made the key contact with Daiwa through Dick's.) Both are still sponsors today. Those two companies were intrigued after the Federation Nationals, and were swayed enough by my Classic performance to come on board. For real money, too, not just product. The Iaconelli Machine was rolling.

As an infant, learning my classic screams in 1973.

On the dock of the cabin in the Poconos in 1974, learning to love the water.

With Pop in 1975, thinking, "Wow I wish I could catch fish like that."

In the old red rental boat with our first trolling motor in 1978. Heading out for a day of trout fishing with Uncle and Pop.

My first really big stringer
of fish, in 1980, including a
nice pickerel. Note Pop's
famous green box on the
picnic table.

Me with Grandmom in 1983,
and one of the first bass I
ever caught.

My first bass over five pounds,
1984. I'm really hooked on bassin'
now. Notice the patches on the
jacket.

Although I'm totally into hockey, fishing, and breakdancing, I still found time
to try out freestyle BMX, 1985.

Me and Mom at my 8th grade graduation dance, in 1986. Nice gray tux!

My first two bass over 6 pounds, in 1988. They were caught on the same day at Fairview Lake in the Poconos.

Senior trip right before graduating Triton in 1990. With, from left
to right, Don Rounon, Steve Pellegrino, Mike Richardson,
and John McGraw.

Three of the original Top Rod members at our club trip to Lake Champlain in 1991.
Left to right: Chris Dalfonso and Steve Pellegrino (aka "the lost member").

Club Buddy tournament for Top Rod Bassmasters with my uncle in 1992. Notice how the small boat was customized to look like a mini bass boat.

Pop sitting on the porch of Cabin #1 in the Poconos, in 1992. Even at his age, he can't wait to go out trout fishing!

Taking a ride in my new bass boat in 1994. I didn't know you could go this fast on the water. This was taken just after I won the 1995 BASS Top 100 tournament as an amateur.

Still with my club Top Rod Bassmasters, in 1995, but starting to feel the need to move up to the next level.

At college graduation in 1997 with my mom and grandmother. Boy, were they proud!

Me at my favorite lake, Alloway Lake, in 1997, with my first fish over 8 pounds. The lake has since been drained and no longer exists.

Me at the BASS Invitational on Lake Martin in 1998. I placed 5th and this gave me enough points to qualify to fish the pro tour in 1999.

Me with my first child, Drew,
a few months after her birth in spring 1999.
What an amazing feeling it is to have a
beautiful, healthy little girl.

My first big National win in May 1999. This was at the BASS Federation Nationals on the Red River. This is the biggest tournament you can win as an amateur fisherman. Winning this qualified me to fish the 1999 Bassmaster Classic.

At the second major event I ever fished as a professional angler, the September 1999 Bassmaster Top 150 on Lake Champlain. Winning this gave me some financial stability at a very unstable time!

Getting dressed to go out to a Halloween party in 2000. I'm dressed up as a pimp, with authentic gold lamé pants and black fur jacket.

Taking a break at a local summer concert called the Rolling Rock Festival held in Latrobe, PA, in 2001.

Me at my second major win, the 2002 BASS Tour event on Seminole in Bambridge, GA. This win was important because it proved I wasn't a fluke.

Me with my two girls at Easter in 2002. It's tough being on the road fishing, and I cherish every moment with my girls.

Hoisting the Classic trophy over my head just seconds after being declared the winner in 2003. What an amazing feeling. Looking down, the first people I saw were my uncle, mom, and grandmother. Oh yes, and the trophy weighed 56 pounds!

At an autograph session right after my Classic win. It was at this point that I realized what kind of platform I would have to help promote the sport of bass fishing!

At my Classic win party in 2003, thrown by my good friend Tim Roach (pictured behind me). The five guys pictured here all traveled together during our semi-pro days. From left to right: Mark Schafer, Jeff Hippert, Tim Roach, Pete Gluszek, and Bob Soley.

In South America filming a TV show in 2003. I had never fished for Peacock Bass before. I'm pictured holding a 14.7 pound Peacock Bass. Wow, what an amazing fight!

Me and John McGraw, on my first official vacation since winning the Classic in August 2003. In Cancun, Mexico, during Spring Break 2004. Am I 31 or 21?

Me and the girls after a busy 2003/2004 season in September 2004. The best gift in the world is to pass on my love of fishing to my two girls, pictured here with a 5-pound-plus bass caught by Rylie. They each caught over 30 bass at the Disney Lakes in Florida.

18 RYLIE IS BORN

When Kristi and I found out she was pregnant again, I was just as excited as the first time. Maybe it stems from being an only child, but I want a large family. I have two beautiful girls right now, and if I never have another child, I'll be perfectly happy. But honestly, I want more kids. I want a litter, to spread my genes everywhere! So a second child was amazing news. Since this was our second pregnancy, we knew the drill better (i.e., no Lamaze this time!). Being there for the birth was again a priority. I didn't want to miss a moment. Kristi was due right around Memorial Day at the end of May in 2000. All I had on my plate around then was practice for the 2000 Classic on Lake Michigan at the end of June. So we were good to go . . . until BASS made an announcement that rocked my world.

"Practice for the 2000 Bassmaster Classic in Chicago will be moved to the first week in June."

Were they kidding? They didn't just do that to me! But then I calmed down, remembering that second pregnancies are never late. This wasn't scientific data, mind you, just something I convinced myself was fact. Plus, my mom, Kristi, Kristi's friends, and everyone else kept telling me what I wanted to hear. "You'll be okay. Don't worry about it. Sometimes second pregnancies even go early." No dice. May came to an end, no baby. I asked, only half kidding, if the doctor might induce labor, something generally reserved for emergencies. Hello! Doesn't Classic practice qualify? I've always maintained it's the most important week of the year for an angler, where he develops his plan to win it all. I had a good chance to do some damage, since Lake Michigan was up north and almost felt like home turf. But Kristi showed no signs of popping. Just like I did when Drew was born, I waited with her until the very last minute. Then Kristi told me to go, and everyone started rooting for a late delivery. So my uncle Don and I took off. Around midnight, we reached Pittsburgh, a little over six hours from New Jersey, and my cell rang. Kristi was in labor!

Need proof that the fishing gods have a sick sense of humor? Pittsburgh is exactly the same distance away from home as Buggs Island, where I had to leave when Drew was born, just in a different direction. How screwed up is that? The whole thing felt like the movie *Groundhog Day.* Nothing left to do but turn around and white-knuckle it at 100 mph back to Jersey with a boat trailing in back. Finally, I pulled into the ER. *Screeecchhhh!* Five hours later, on June 3, 2000, Rylie Nicole Iaconelli came into the world, with me at Kristi's bedside. Another amazing experience. Once again, I stayed with Kristi and the baby until late morning, missed a day of practice, then raced back. And just like before, I couldn't have cared less about the missed day. All I could think about was my new little girl.

Fatherhood

I've loved every minute of being Drew and Rylie's father, the good and bad. The simple things, from watching them color to changing their diapers, have always been my favorite. Yeah, being on the road so much means I miss a lot of the daily grind, but the flip side is I miss a lot of the proud moments, too. It's hard being away so much, but I'm thankful for everything I've been a part of, and fortunately, I've seen a lot. Watching Drew go to the potty for the first time. Seeing them take their first steps. Firsts always blow my mind. I also love seeing how the simple things get them so excited (just like Daddy). They'll become fascinated with a day-old muffin, wondering how the blueberries got in there. That attitude toward the world and its endless possibilities is how I try to approach my life and my fishing. Everything is new and beautiful. I hope they never lose that quality.

19 THE BAD SEASON

i *The Worst News Ever*

I often refer to the 2000–2001 season as "my bad season." It was nothing but mediocre to bad finishes, and the only year I missed the Classic since turning pro. But it wasn't just my performance on the water that made it a nightmare. For about six months before the season started, Uncle Don was suffering through a constant, vicious flu. Sore throat. Runny nose. Coughing. He kept taking over-the-counter medicine, but couldn't completely kick it. Still, he didn't think it was serious, so it kept lingering. Finally, Don gave in and went to get checked out, to pick up a flu shot or antibiotic. His doctor wasn't overly concerned, but set up a blood test just in case. That's when he learned it wasn't the flu, but something far worse. Hodgkin's disease.

Don was diagnosed right before I was about to leave for a big tournament, and my family didn't want to upset me before I left. So they waited until I got back to tell me he had cancer. It was yet another example of them making me their first priority. Even when they told me, they downplayed the situation, focusing on how relatively curable Hodgkin's is compared to other cancers. Only after Don was in remission did I learn his Hodgkin's lymphoma was actually fourth stage, where the odds of survival drop considerably. But they didn't want to distract me during my season.

Don's illness was hardly the sole cause for my struggles. I just wasn't fishing that well. But his battles with chemo and radiation lingered in the back of my mind. I never outwardly showed it, but I was really scared. I thought, "He can't go. There's just no way Don can leave." I would never use his situation as an excuse for my poor performance, but not knowing what was going to happen was killing me inside, which affected my '00–'01 season, for sure.

Sucking Left and Right

I had a run of bad tournaments, like dominoes falling one after the other. By the end of 2001 I had strung together three or four bad finishes and actually debated quitting, going back to Dick's or enrolling in school again. All the stuff happening to my uncle made me feel detached about my career. I had already accomplished nearly every goal I had set for myself. I came up through the Federation ranks to make the tours. I'd won a major on the BASS trail. I'd fished two Classics. I'd have nothing to be ashamed about if I called it quits. Still, despite my slump, with a decent finish at Douglas Lake in Tennessee, the last tournament of the season, I would have a legitimate shot of making the Classic. But everything that could have gone wrong did. I lost fish at the side of my boat. I broke my line. My mind was being pulled in a million directions, I had never felt so much pressure in a tournament, and I completely buckled.

Worse, my mouth again got me in trouble. A few months before, I'd done an interview with Tim Tucker from *Bassmaster* magazine, where I said, "I don't want to sound conceited when I say this, but making the Classic anymore, I don't see that being a problem for me at all. . . . My real thing I'm trying for every year is Angler of the Year now. Between the Invitationals and the Top 150s, I expect to make the Classic every year, and if I don't, I'll be super, super disappointed in my performance." That upset a lot of anglers, even friends like Skeet. It sounded like my ego was out of control, because making the Classic year in and year out is difficult. Most guys can't do it, and they probably felt like I was still a little green to be talking that kind of smack. All I meant was that I have really high standards for myself. I expect to *win* the Classic every year, not just qualify. I wasn't trying to put anyone down, because I knew qualifying for the event wasn't easy. That point was driven home when my wipeout at Douglas Lake ensured I'd miss the 2001 Classic. Now I was eating crow. It was that domino effect, negatives breeding negatives, and I felt like there was no light at the end of the tunnel.

Don's Remission

Fishing has always helped me deal with situations I can't control, like Don's sickness. On the water, I call it the "uncontrollable factor." I can study maps, spool my line, sharpen my hooks, and execute every cast at the perfect angle. That's all within my control. But when my motor blows up because of a faulty power head, or when ten other anglers found the spot I hoped I'd have to myself, or weather changes the fishing conditions, what can I do about that? Those are the uncontrollables, which I can't worry about because they're not within my power to change. I'm learning to accept it and apply these lessons to everyday life. Don's illness was an uncontrollable. I'm not the most devout Christian in the world, but I prayed a lot while Don was sick, telling God I'd trade my success in a heartbeat if Don got better. It would all be meaningless without him around.

I tried to stay optimistic. He got through his chemotherapy

treatments without losing a stitch of his big, shaggy Beatles haircut, which is pretty rare, and I took it as a good sign. But you still never know. So when we finally got the news that Don was in remission, I went nuts with joy. I can't begin to describe my relief. And not coincidentally, I quickly broke out of my slump. Without a doubt, Don deserves 100 percent of the credit. I compared my lousy fishing to Don's near-death experience. He fought for months, but not once did I see him feeling sorry for himself. He never changed, which blew me away. If he could face cancer without complaining, where did I get off moaning about some bad tournaments? He motivated me to kick butt the following season. It didn't take long for me to get back on track.

Misguided Thanks

I started 2002 with a bang by winning the Georgia Open at Lake Seminole. The old Ike was back and my slump was officially over. And just as I dedicated my win on Lake Champlain to my grandfather, that second major was in honor of my uncle. Ironically, that caused a little trouble. Our immediate family and close friends were aware of Don's illness, but my uncle, mom, and grandmom are private people, and would have preferred the fishing community remain out of the loop. I wouldn't say they were angry when I went public with the news, but they weren't thrilled, either. But I wanted people to know what this victory was about, and why I was motivated again. I honestly didn't realize it would bother them. It's all water under the bridge by now. Uncle Don is still doing great. He even traveled with me during the '04 season.

20 CONTINUING EVOLUTION

ESPN

Things weren't looking up just for me. When ESPN purchased BASS in 2001, it was a lifesaver for us. The organization had flatlined under the old regime of Helen Sevier and Dewey "Napoleon" Kendrick, but ESPN helped create huge opportunities, with big increases in prize money and exposure for the sport. I think ESPN watched the explosion of NASCAR, a sport with the same southern roots as bass fishing, and saw a similar opportunity for success. For better or worse, ESPN has a huge impact on what sports are popular. Look at the X Games or the Great Outdoor Games, where they created a market for sports that didn't have major media outlets. But ESPN represented change, and in the beginning, they had a lot of critics who wanted to preserve "what was working." But what was working, when the number of fifteen- to thirty-year-olds entering the sport had been declining steadily for years? People just weren't interested anymore, and that needed to change. Others complained because ESPN was turning BASS into a big media production. Exactly! That's the whole point! People will watch it and the sport will grow. Then there were the idiots crying, "ESPN is only changing stuff so they can make more money." So what? They're a business. Like Helen Sevier didn't want to make a profit? The final straw for some old schoolers? ESPN is headquartered in Bristol, Connecticut. Not exactly Dixie. But how do you argue with narrow-minded people? It's impossible.

I'm not saying the transition has been all peachy keen. When ESPN first bought BASS, they didn't realize the Federation was the backbone of the organization and debated taking away the Federation entries into the Classic, which nearly caused an uprising. The Federation was ready to quit and move over to FLW, and I agreed with them. They were right. But ESPN realized they screwed up, and didn't just correct the mistake, but went a step further and made an improvement. BASS is launching a whole new tournament program for weekend anglers called the Bassmasters Weekend Series, a trail of eighty tournaments whose winner will qualify for the 2006 Classic. So not only has ESPN listened to concerns regarding the Federation, they took a bigger step toward helping the everyday club fisherman with the twelve-foot johnboat. That tends to be how they operate. When ESPN makes a mistake, they work to fix it.

INFORMATION EXPLOSION

When ESPN purchased BASS, the amount of exposure the sport received, through increased tournament coverage and groundbreaking shows like *BASSCenter,* was huge, and gave lots of information to anglers everywhere. But they were just continuing a trend that had been going on for a while. The TV and video explosion of the eighties had people taking a more intellectual approach to fishing, treating information as a more valuable commodity. The landmark Bassmaster University program, which started around the same time, meant amateurs could enroll in courses taught by pros, exposing themselves to huge new bodies of information. This took years off our learning curve. When the Internet exploded, it opened even more doors. With such easy access to vast amounts of data on the Web, a twelve-year-old in 2005 can learn ten times faster than I could at the same age. Pros have Web sites with articles that can be instantly downloaded. I would have killed for the other programs available for today's youth too. Casting Kids is the pioneer, getting kids involved through casting competitions. They cast, flip, and pitch like young football fans punt, pass, and kick. Then there's the Junior Chapter Program, which creates clubs for thirteen- to fifteen-year-olds. Back in the day, you had to be at least sixteen to join a club, and youth chapters were nonexistent.

Some older guys get upset that the new generation can learn so fast. That's just sour grapes, worrying some kid's gonna take his spot and sponsors. Screw that! Everyone should be excited, because a whole generation of quality anglers has been created. I have no problem spilling the beans about my techniques and strategies for turning pro on my audio CD, or teaching people what I've learned about finding sponsors. I *want* new blood in there, and look forward to being knocked out of the box. It won't be easy for the newbies. Older guys like Denny who embrace change still kick my butt all the time. Gary Klein is a veteran whose strengths are pitching and flipping. But when the West Coast guys started kicking butt with drop shotting, he went out of his way to learn it. During an FLW tournament where he missed the cut, he followed Aaron Martins all day, watching this new kid drop shot. That showed he's not scared of the future. By embracing it, he strengthens his own fishing. That's why he's stayed on top for so long.

CHANGE JUST AIN'T POPULAR

I'm not saying all change is for the better, but there are too many guys who automatically see it as "the end of our gentleman's sport as we know it." No way! Fishing has evolved, becoming more of a spectator sport, with bigger personalities. But at its core, it's the same sport. It's just not solely "theirs" anymore, which all those close-minded Bubbas hate. They've had to give up a bit to hip-hoppers from New Jersey. Or California. Or African-American anglers like Ish Monroe, or even Japanese fishermen like Takahiro Omori. But that's a victory for fishing. It means our sport has global popularity. I have no problem getting my butt kicked by any angler from anywhere in the world, if he's good and can help blow bass fishing into the mainstream. There are some women, too, on the FLW tour.

It's sad, but Takahiro winning the 2004 Classic generated a lot of smack talk in chat rooms and fan boards. That he shouldn't be fishing because he's not American. He didn't take his victory lap with an American flag like everyone else usually does. (He also didn't have a Japanese flag, or any flag for that matter.) But what's the problem? He just won the Classic, for God's sake! He can do what he wants. I'm sure you could dig up some offensive trash on the Internet about Ish, too, since he's a black angler. But let me be clear: this ignorance *does not* come from the professionals. Every pro I know thought T.O.'s win was amazing. The junk comes from the wannabes and negative fans. Even the pros fearing change know what it takes to win a Classic, and how T.O. busted his butt for over ten years on the circuit for his chance. And that's after he came to America not knowing a lick of English. They respect how he smoked the field on Lake Wylie. We know the truth, and most fans are great people who love bass fishing, no matter what race, creed, or color the angler might be. It's that small minority left over that can kiss it.

21 THE PERFECT STORM

In 2002, I arrived at the Saint Lawrence River and Lake Ontario for the BASS New York Northern Open, needing a Top 10 finish to qualify for the 2003 Classic through the Invitationals. On my first day, the weather was beautiful. Crystal clear skies, with smooth water. I managed to find some quality concentrations of smallmouths and had a solid day. But on Day Two, I wanted to reach a spot on Lake Ontario about thirty-eight miles from the launch, where I thought I could get more weight. As I approached the mouth of the big lake, the slow, rolling waves started growing, and growing, until they were nearly ten feet high. It was a horrible feeling, and then I noticed I was the only boat going into the mouth of the lake. Everyone else was moving in the opposite direction. I exchanged looks with my amateur riding with me as we both thought, "That's not a good sign!" This was the abyss. At that point, I had to make a decision. Did I trust my boat-handling skills enough to keep going, or should I turn around with all the other guys? I was scared, and my white-knuckled amateur had probably crapped himself. His life was in my hands, and I'm sure he figured if we kept going, he was a dead man.

Screw it! I'm going in!

I made a hard left toward my target area, and headed into the troughs between the waves. Now that we'd entered Ontario, the waves were ten and twelve feet high. Just thinking about negotiating those nasty waves in a flat, open bass boat is completely terrifying. I was trying to stay in the troughs. All I could see were walls of water on each side as the rest of the world disappeared. But as always, I was ultra-prepared. I have an extra bilge pump mounted on the floor of my boat, which I always keep running. It can pump out one thousand gallons at capacity, so all the water coming in over the sides was shot back out by the pump. All my electronics were off the boat, except my GPS, but that's mounted in the dash, so a rush of water can't break it off. Most important, I drove the boat perfectly. I even conquered the mother of all waves, probably thirteen or fourteen feet high, making a great move to turn with the crest. But water still rolled over the front of the boat and ripped the trolling motor off the deck! But being a spare parts kinda guy, I had another stowed away. I just kept going, concentrating on every wave as it rolled past.

We finally reached my spot, which was protected and calm. It took about twenty minutes to replace the trolling motor, especially with my hands shaking like a leaf. But once I started casting, all my nerves disappeared. I caught sixteen pounds in forty-five minutes! That's just sick! Unfortunately, forty-five minutes was all I had, because I had to leave myself three hours to travel the tough water back to the dock. I was toast by the end of the day, and when I reached the dock, everyone was shaking his head. My body, my boat, and my passenger were all soaked, and you could tell I'd been through hell. Even Woo Daves, an old, laid-back vet who has seen everything, was amazed. He just looked at me, laughed, and said, "You crazy, boy!" I smiled to myself. "Woo Daves thinks I'm crazy! How cool is that!" Maybe he was right, but those sixteen pounds helped me to a ninth-place finish, which was enough to qualify me for the 2003 Classic, which I won. My decision to conquer the high seas had paid off big-time.

22 IT'S OVER

Divorce

In March, only a couple of months before the practice period for the '03 Classic, my marriage had, for all intents and purposes, officially ended. Done. I ended up tossing my wedding ring in Timber Creek, a branch of the Delaware that runs behind my uncle's house, which is where the ring remains to this day. As far as I was concerned, Mike Iaconelli was single, end of story.

But deep down inside, the situation was killing me. I mean, Kristi was my girl since freakin' high school! Yeah, we had periods of on-again, off-again, but there were also periods that were amazing. She seemed to understand and even accept that fishing was my future. But from the moment we exchanged vows, we were in trouble, whether we knew it or not. The weird thing was, once we were married, there weren't any "Mike, it's fishing or me" confrontations. No "Mike, I'm really having a problem with you going," or "Mike, I'm feeling lonely and left out." It felt like one day, Kristi just unloaded all this frustration, and everything went to pieces.

THE SIGNS

Truthfully, this didn't happen overnight. Looking back, there were times when subconsciously I realized things were heading south, even if I wasn't willing to acknowledge it. When I won that Lake Seminole tournament in 2002, I had an FLW event on Lake Wheeler the next week, which meant I had to go straight to practice. So I called her from the road. "Kristi! I just won my second major! $110,000!" When I won that first major at Lake Champlain, it felt like Kristi was just as happy as me. But this time, her reaction was different. It felt almost like she didn't care. Something was off, I could tell. But like a dum-dum, I just filed it away. I didn't want to see any trouble coming.

But there were times I should have seen it, and at the 2002 Classic on Lay Lake in Birmingham, trouble finally arrived. Kristi traveled with me, which was noteworthy because she didn't do that a lot. Once the tournament started, I got into the traditional, uncanny pattern I have in Classics of amazing first days, jackass second days, then good third days that are too little, too late (there's one exception, of course). That's exactly how it went in Birmingham. As usual, I was really hard on myself, which was always a major issue with Kristi. I was angry, she was angry that I was angry, and that tension hit the breaking point on the way back to Jersey. We had a huge blowout. Kristi said she couldn't stand me being gone and didn't feel the same about me anymore. Then I totally flipped out. We laid everything out on the table, no holds barred.

I threatened to pack my bags and move out. In the meantime, I took the kids down to the shore in Ocean City. I needed to be alone, away from Kristi. But after a little bit, she ended up joining us, and we talked things over. By that point, the problems weren't solved, but we got a better handle on the other's point of view. She got everything off her chest, which wasn't easy to do. It's hard to be that honest sometimes. I was shocked that all these issues had built up for Kristi.

NO MORE HOLDING BACK

We saw a counselor and did the normal stuff people do to repair a relationship. But the big problem was almost unsolvable: fishing. The idea of me quitting kept coming up. In all honesty, I don't think she truly wanted me to quit. It's more like she wanted me to stop without stopping, to fish competitively without the competitive fishing lifestyle, but that was impossible. Kristi wanted me to be successful and happy, but she just hated the setup. Every time I did well, Kristi knew I'd be gone even longer. The more success I had, the worse it was for her.

But I was still mad, because from day one I suggested traveling together. Drew hadn't even started kindergarten yet. The kids could have gone with us. But truthfully, Kristi likes to work, and had no interest in being an angler's wife on the road. She wanted to start her own salon, so I said, "Cool," and bought it for her. I figured, "That's her baby. It'll help her focus her energy during my time away." But really the salon hurt, because once Kristi had her business, it was even harder for her to travel, in spite of our financial stability. From the moment I won that first major and the hundred grand that went with it, she was essentially working for baby money. But she enjoyed it, and it was only fair, since I got to do what made me happy, too. I don't resent that. But I always knew if you didn't travel with your wife, girlfriend, significant other, or whatever title you're giving her, it wouldn't work. The lifestyle would always defeat the relationship. Of course, I always thought I'd be the exception to the rule.

If Kristi had told me this when it first became an issue, back in 1999 or 2000, maybe we'd have found a compromise. I could have skipped the FLWs and just fished BASS events. I could have fished fewer practice days. But she never said anything. I understand how Kristi's mindset could have changed. The load seemed smaller three years earlier. It wasn't unreasonable for her to change her mind as my schedule took me away for longer stretches. Maybe I didn't notice, because we'd been together so long and I thought she was comfortable with the drill. Plus, she had a base in New Jersey, between her family, friends, and business. It's not like she was sitting at home, waiting around for me all day. And she had said, "It's okay. Go for it!" What else was I supposed to think? Who knows? Maybe I was just gone too much to see how unhappy she was.

TWO TO TANGO

I'm blasting her for not coming clean, but there was a laundry list of issues I didn't own up to, either. I didn't like how she kept the house. She didn't cook. She wasn't the best "homemaker" in general. But I justified everything, because she put up with the lifestyle of an angler's wife. Even though "this, this, and this" weren't the way I liked it, she was making a big sacrifice, too. She'd been with me since day one. I'd deal with it. Looking back, I was doing exactly what she was. Keeping secrets. It was like we both knew we couldn't say what we really felt and stay married.

Between March and June, I asked myself the same question over and over a million times: "Would things have been different if I put the relationship first and got another job?" I could have been in advertising. I could have been a teacher. During this major mental breakdown, my answer was always, "It could have been different, you dumbass! Why did you insist on having your cake and eating it, too?" But now, 99 percent of the time, my answer to the same question is "No. It was doomed from the beginning." If I were a teacher, or a postman, or tripping over boxes at Accumark, we'd still have divorced. I watched my cousin Jen's "perfect" marriage bite the bullet after ten years. She was a loving housewife with a husband who worked a nine-to-five job. Kristi and I would have been doomed either way. Fishing just sped up the process. Just as I always believe in things being meant to be, the opposite is sometimes just as inevitable, too.

FINDING A BRIGHT SIDE

My biggest worries when Kristi and I broke up were Drew and Rylie. Kids love routine. For some, that's Dad coming home at five, hanging with them till they go to bed at nine, getting them off to school the next day, then coming back at five. But in our family, it was never like that, so luckily, in a lot of ways, nothing changed for them. After the breakup, their routines remained the same. I still see them when I'm home from tournaments. When I'm gone, I talk to them on the phone two or three times a week. That's what the girls have known their whole lives.

Kristi and I don't do holidays together anymore, and that's hard for the girls. Frankly, Kristi and I aren't in the same place at the same time too often. And obviously, "Who's this dude?" questions come up if she's seeing someone, and "Who's this girl?" with me. It isn't traumatizing now, but eventually we'll have to explain, "This is Daddy's friend. This is Mommy's friend. But Daddy's still Daddy and Mommy's still Mommy." The toughest parts are yet to come. Hopefully, it won't be too painful. Kristi and I have worked hard not to use the kids as pawns when we're angry at each other. We're both very conscious of that. And it's not like she pulls that Jerry Springer stuff. Kristi's not a bad person. Most important, she's a great mom to my girls.

People always talk about learning and growing from their failures. That's definitely something positive that's happened from all this. If there's an issue in my relationships now, I bring it to the table and let the woman know. If the situation isn't totally perfect, it ain't worth it to me. Well, nothing's totally perfect, but you know what I mean.

23

2003 CLASSIC

The Last Hoorah

Between March and the official practice of the Bassmaster Classic in June, I was worthless. My life was crashing and burning. I couldn't focus on anything but my breakup and everything that came with it. My life had hit an absolute low and didn't look like it was getting better anytime soon. I felt screwed. Angry. Bitter. That's when you start looking to shift the blame. I had to pin my misery on something, so I picked the easiest scapegoat I could find: fishing.

After all, fishing was the reason I was in this mess, right? If I had just gotten a normal job that made me happy enough, Kristi and I would have been blessed with a problem-free marriage. Perfect harmony. Bliss. Please! I realize now that's all complete nonsense. But as I headed to New Orleans to practice on the Delta, my mind was going in circles and

I was thinking irrationally. Which is why I decided to do something completely insane.

I decided to quit fishing.

I was washing my hands of the whole sport. Over and out. I was done. My plan was to fish the biggest bass-fishing tournament in the world, then ride off into the sunset and not look back. I was dead serious. This was my last Classic. My last tournament. My last everything.

The Stupidest Plan of My Life

I started breaking down my fishing-free future. I couldn't just *quit working*. I needed to make a living. So where do I always end up after quitting a job? Back to school! This time, I'd actually finish my teaching degree. I already had two semesters of work toward my postbaccalaureate program. So what if nearly six years had passed? I called Rowan and set up a date in August for an admittance test. In the meantime, I'd go back and work at Dick's part-time. I wasn't dying to get back into retail, but I needed a practical way to save some money before school started. Eventually, I'd become a full-time teacher and be a regular guy like everyone else. Problem solved.

Maybe a small part of me was attempting to salvage my marriage by doing the "right" things. But I don't think that was it. By this point there were things said and done between Kristi and me that moved us beyond the point of no return. Divorce was a given. This was about not letting fishing screw up my next relationship. I needed to start over and do it right this time.

I barely told anyone outside of my mom, my uncle, my grandma, and Pete. My family didn't hammer me with a billion questions. They just wanted to make sure I had given it enough thought. My mom always said that I'd be a great teacher, anyway. To them, I could do anything I wanted. But this was a drastic decision. I was taking a goal I had worked at, on some level, since I was twelve, and literally tossing it away forever. They wanted to make sure I wasn't doing something I might regret. But at the same time, my family wouldn't stand in my way. They've been totally supportive my entire life, and this was no different.

STILL A SERIOUS MISSION

This'll sound weird, but even after deciding to break clean from the sport that wrecked my life, I was still totally motivated to win in New Orleans. It wasn't about a desire to further my career, beat the fish, or prove I belonged. All I wanted was to go out in style. This was my last chance to make my mark on the biggest stage BASS has to offer. I wanted to take from fishing as much as it took from me. Winning for the sake of winning. The visions were clear in my head. "This is your fourth and last Classic. Let's go out and win this!"

Fueled by sadness and spite, I prepared for the Classic like any other tournament. My notes from the '99 Classic held up very well, so I just added any updated information about the Delta I could find in newer magazines and photographs. I decided there were really only three areas where anyone had the potential to win: Venice, Bayou Black, and Bayou Buff, where Davy Hite won the '99 Classic. I figured there'd be way too many people following Davy to the Buff after his success there. Then I decided there was no reason to hit Venice when I knew Bayou Black like the back of my hand. Plus, a hurricane had blown through the Delta that winter, and since they usually pummel the coastal areas, it would have wrecked Venice. This made Bayou Black seem even more inviting. I could win it all in Bayou Black. I'm *gonna* win it all in Bayou Black! That knowledge of the area and my confidence got me psyched up for a good practice, even though I was still depressed as I drove down to New Orleans with my uncle.

BAYOU BLACK

Unfortunately, my research needed overhauling from minute one. The hurricane took some strange turns, striking hard inland near Bayou

Black but completely missing Venice. Still, I thought Bayou Black was the ticket. I spent the first day with my uncle in the Orange Grove, one of my favorite sections of the Black . . . and caught nothing! Not a thing! If you think I was in a bad mood then . . .

You should have seen me on Day Two. I hit some fringe areas around Bayou Black and caught a whopping six-pound limit! Six pounds? That's not even heavy for a newborn! Six pounds definitely wouldn't cut it in the Classic. The hurricane had completely devastated the fishing environment in Bayou Black. I had struck out in my first two practice days, and was seriously frustrated.

I needed a change, so I threw up my hands, packed up my Suburban, and headed off to Venice. I didn't have hotel reservations in Venice. I had never been to Venice. I wasn't even positive how to *get* to Venice. But launching there rather than from Bayou Black saved three hours of riding time getting to my practice spots. I checked into some motel over there at about one in the morning. This felt like the right plan. Even if the bags in Bayou Black somehow got up to eight or nine pounds, better than either practice day, it wouldn't be nearly enough. I had to start over.

STILL SUCKING IN VENICE

On the third practice day, I focused on three spots in Venice that I had found on the aerial photos I uncovered during my research. The first section was an area called "Old Dennis," which had clear water, current, and vegetation. Second was the area around Venice Marina, and my last priority was an area called Delta Duck. I wanted to spend a day in each fishery, then expand and define the best one on my sixth and last day of practice. Unfortunately, I also had to learn where I was on the water, no easy task in a huge fishery where everything looks identical. Once I found Old Dennis, I ended plucking out around twelve pounds, which smoked Bayou Black. I actually felt pretty stoked, like I was finally on a roll. I was so happy to finally be on some fish, I decided to tweak my plan for Day Four. Instead of hitting Venice Marina like I'd planned, I decided to go back to Old Dennis and define it.

What a dum-dum! When I came back to Old Dennis the next day, the tide was way higher, and the raised water level totally messed with the fish. When the water rises, the bass and the baitfish have more space to spread out. The bass will head deeper into the cover, and spread themselves out in pursuit of a good meal. By the time I said "screw it" and hit Venice Marina, I had only half a day to explore, which wasn't nearly enough. I hooked a few small ones, but nothing significantly better than Old Dennis. And without enough time to really check out the area, Day Four ended up a complete waste of time.

ROCK BOTTOM

By the time Day Five rolled around, I still had no handle on a winning spot, and was running out of time to figure it out. I decided to spend the day in the Delta Duck. The *whole* day this time. If that didn't work, I'd learn Old Dennis on the last practice day and make that area my primary pattern. End of story.

I arrived in the Duck full of optimism . . . and barely had a bite (so what else is new?). By 12 or 1 P.M., the puny six-pound bag from my first day in Bayou Black was looking fatter than Santa's sack. I felt like bailing, but had already learned my lesson after ruining Day Four rushing through the Venice Marina. I was better off sticking it out in the Duck. Besides, how much worse could it get?

Cue the vicious, horrendous, sky-turning-green-and-black storm! Ugly. Menacing. Wind, torrential rain, and lightning bolts were crashing down around us, and there was nowhere to hide. Delta Duck, like the rest of the Delta, has virtually no cover. It's all low marsh, reeds, and canals, a big maze of nothing.

There was no point in taking off. Even if we tried outrunning the storm, which was impossible, we had no clue where we were. We would have just driven around aimlessly in the rain. All I could do was jam the boat into the reeds and use the tall, reedy roseau cane to create a sort of ghetto canopy. It wasn't actual cover, but it was better than nothing. If I huddled up on the front deck and used whatever shelter the plants could give me, maybe it would take fifteen minutes to get drenched instead of five. My uncle just said "screw it," stayed in his chair, and got wet. But I was messed up emotionally, at the end of my rope. My stress level had never been higher as I curled into a ball on the front deck. Then, somehow, I fell asleep.

Mr. Sandman

This wasn't normal. I've never ever, ever, *ever,* in my entire life, fallen asleep while fishing. Never. I don't remember passing out, or even dreaming, but I was down for the count for at least half an hour, maybe forty minutes. My mind, my body, my heart, and my soul reached the exhaustion point and needed to check out for a while, you know what I mean?

When I woke up, the storm was gone. The worst had passed, and I felt totally refreshed, like when you open your eyes from a nap with your batteries recharged. Except I had just unloaded months of stress. I unzipped my rain jacket, straightened up my equipment, and refocused. It was almost two-thiry, I hadn't caught jack, and it was time to fish.

24 BACK TO WORK

Heart of Darkness

During my research, this tiny pond stuck out on my aerial maps like Disneyland, the Happiest Place on Earth. I called it "the Heart," because current and wind drained water through these different "valves," creating beautiful flows of water through its heartlike shape. It was a perfect tidal presence, and even better, the Heart was a pitch-black hole in the photograph, which meant it had superclear water! This is where the baitfish and vegetation would be, which meant the bass would be there too.

The only problem? I couldn't figure out where the hell it was. The whole thing was the size of Hershey Lake back in Jersey, maybe five acres. Trying to find an entrance into this tiny spot was like looking for a needle in a haystack. For the life of me, I couldn't figure out how to get in there. The good buzz from my nap was fading. We were heading down a canal, and the water was a hideous shade of muddy brown. Nothing like the aerials. I was totally confused. Soon the water started clearing up, but the canal was growing more narrow. I watched the wall of reeds close in around me until it nearly touched the sides of the boat. I came off pad, brought it down to an idle, and that's when I saw it. The most amazing thing I'd seen in months. Beautiful, black, clear water. As in aerial-map black! It was exactly what I wanted. The hall of reeds opened up, and the Heart was right in front of me. I had made it!

Xanadu

My uncle and I looked like slack-jawed idiots as the current pulled us into the clear, open water. Mullet, a Delta species that for no apparent reason will leap up to ten feet out of the water, were all over the place. *Whoosh!* Then they'd hit the water and do it all over again. My uncle and I didn't say a word. We just picked up our rods and started casting. The first five casts, nothing. Then my uncle hooked a five-pounder. After three more casts, I snagged a three-pounder. Only a few hours later, we had eighteen or nineteen pounds apiece. *Apiece!* That perfect tide, almost dead low, pushed the fish to the edges of the Heart, where food was plentiful. Ideal tidal conditions! Clear water! Totally hidden from other anglers! This was it! This was the spot where I could win the 2003 Bassmaster Classic.

We bailed just before the sun went down. To make sure I'd find my way back quickly and easily, I marked every turn and twist along the route, leaving a GPS breadcrumb trail. Finally, I had no doubt what my next day's plan would be. I had a one-track mind, to expand and define the Duck.

Plucking the Duck

When I arrived at the Duck on Day Five, it was at dead low tide, but it had risen to dead high tide by Day Six. Only twelve hours after smoking them, the bites weren't coming. That uneasy feeling started boiling back to the surface, but once I settled down and focused, I realized I had an opportunity to find my sweet spot. I knew this concentration of fish spent their entire life cycle in this tidal pond. It had deep and shallow water, current, and loads of great forage. Those bass weren't going anywhere. If I could trigger the bites in a lousy tide, I could do it anytime.

The roseau cane was too vertical and dense to fish effectively, so I keyed in on these tidal flats with little sediment buildups at their mouths. At high tide, most of the fish set up shop on these little flats, moving up as the water level rose. That's where I could nab them. Learning that, plus having the whole day to play with different baits, casts, and line, made me confident I'd catch them no matter what. Even in less ideal conditions, I still caught about fifteen pounds! This spot was absolutely incredible.

I was also confident that I'd have it all to myself. The Delta is so big that places can easily go decades without being fished. I'm willing to bet there are areas in the Delta that still have never seen bait or a boat. It wasn't unrealistic to think I had charted new ground. I hadn't seen a soul there in two days, and the fish were biting like they'd never seen lures in their lives. Unfortunately, you never know for sure. I had found spots in other tournaments and thought, "Ain't nobody finding this baby!" only to get there and find people lined up like they were waiting to buy U2 tickets. You can never be sure . . . but I felt really good.

Looking back, that rainstorm saved my career. I was depressed, getting divorced, and ready to quit. I had fished all over the Delta and found nothing. Then everything was raining down on me, literally and figuratively. I was reduced to shoving my boat into a bunch of reeds. In all honesty, I had given up. If the storm didn't come, I'd have kept fishing, but my mind would have been too cluttered to track down the Heart. I'd have bombed out when the tournament rolled around a month later. Instead, I was forced to stop and let my body shut down. That break stopped the insanity just long enough for me to recover. Like an alcoholic who hits rock bottom, I found my moment of clarity.

Thinking about that moment still gives me chills.

Gonna Take More than That to Stop My Sulking

I had found a winning spot and left Louisiana on a high, but the minute I got back to New Jersey I was right back down in the dumps. I didn't pick up a rod for the entire month between pre-practice and the start of the tournament. Not even for fun fishing. The last thing I wanted to do was pull fish out of the water. I was back on the floor at Dick's and ready to return to Rowan in the fall. I went out drinking every night. I didn't care about fishing. I was aware that I hadn't lost a leg, that my house hadn't been swept up in a flood, and that my kids were safe and healthy. I understood there are things in the world way worse than my divorce, but nonetheless, I had never dealt with so much pain in my life.

Looking back, it's hard to believe I bothered fishing the Classic at all, considering how much my emotions clouded my thinking. But deep down, I still loved the sport. Fishing was my life's passion. I still lived for competition and winning. And I couldn't stop thinking about the Heart. I'd wake up in a cold sweat after dreaming about pulling huge sacks from the pond's clear water. If I really wanted out, why would I be dreaming about the Louisiana Delta? Why would I have done my map work, research, and meticulously prepared my equipment? Why would I even bother torturing myself for one more stupid tournament?

I don't know why that didn't sink in.

25

GAME ON . . .
SORT OF

Heading to the Classic

In August, it was time to hit the Delta. We'd have a single day of practice before the Classic began. The drive to New Orleans from South Jersey takes about twenty-one hours. By myself, I would have done half in one day, stopped overnight, then finished up the next day. But riding with Pete Gluszek meant we could do the whole thing in one shot. The backseat of my Suburban was kept open, so whoever wasn't driving could jump back there for a quick nap if he wanted to. But we ended up talking more than we slept, and not about fishing, which normally dominated these road trip conversations. We focused on the personal problems we were dealing with. Breakups. How fishing, our love and passion, could screw up and cancel out all the good it brings. We went around in circles. I was ping-ponging between "Screw this!" and "Man, I got a good feeling about this tournament!" and Pete kept saying, "Mike, I know what you're going through. In a couple of months, you'll settle down and feel better."

"No, I won't, Pete! Screw this!"

"Hey, that's a good choice, too, Mike. Go back to school. You can still tournament fish on weekends."

He knew what I was feeling, for sure, because he had gone through the same thing. A couple of years earlier his marriage had ended, and Pete was again working through a breakup. He understood, and saw in my eyes that I was serious about bailing.

BOURBON (AND EVERY OTHER BOOZE) STREET

When we finally got to New Orleans, I was still nowhere close to 100 percent focused. Normally before a tournament, I *never* do anything remotely resembling fun, just staying inside and getting room service. This time? Pete and I were hitting Bourbon Street in a daze, getting totally drunk, right up to our day of practice. I was chain-smoking cigarettes and I don't even smoke! Whatever. All bets were off at that point. "This is it, New Orleans!" I thought, "I'm going out a champ, then I ain't letting the back door hit me on the way out!"

GROGGY BUT GROOVY

Waking up at four-thirty with a splitting headache for the final day of practice was a drag. But at the same time, I was relaxed and very content to just fish the moment. I would start in the Heart, and after about an hour make a run back to Old Dennis. If they bit, fantastic. If not, I'd designated Bayou Black as my backup area, and would just fish there. That would be that. There wasn't much time for tinkering, because with a mock weigh-in during the afternoon, the last day is more for BASS and ESPN to work out the logistical kinks of the massive Classic production than it is about fishing. You can't do much more with the day than use it as a tune-up. It reinforces my belief that anglers win the Classic in the official pre-practice a month before we arrive at the tournament. If you're not simply double-checking what you've already learned when you practice during tournament week, you're in trouble.

Ordering off the Menu

In every other major tournament, an angler can load as much gear on his boat as he wants. I could bring one hundred rods and five hundred tackle bags if I thought it'd help. But in the Classic, there's a cap on equipment. Eight rods and reels and two tackle bags. That's it. Ideally, you'd want a good variety of gear to prepare for any situation. But when your choices become that limited, anglers have to think very carefully about what's on their boat. Sometimes, that requires a little assistance.

During the official Classic pre-practice in March, I noticed a lot of bass had bluegill in their guts. Each was three to four inches, olive green with a black back and bright orange belly. Half a dozen puked up the exact same meal. Coincidence? I think not. So back in Jersey, I called Mike McPherson, who runs the bait production and manufacturing department at Mann's Bait Company, and told him what I'd seen. He made me a set of lures—Stone Jigs, spinnerbaits, plastics, etc.—in the same color pattern as the bluegill the fish were eating. I then called Mike back with changes to match the colors even more exactly. "Needs more green. Put a little more orange in the belly." We went back and forth, bouncing ideas and designs off each other like mad angler scientists.

This kind of access and input is a luxury only a handful of professional anglers have. How'd I luck out? For one, Mann's has always respected my interest and skill in lure design. And unlike a bigger company like PRADCO, where the pro staff might be sixty guys worldwide, Mann's, comparatively speaking, is still a Mom and Pop operation. They have maybe five guys on the high-level pro staff, which means easy access to the honchos. Good stuff, since lure design and strategy is yet another way I look to push it to the next level. I could have thrown a standard jig on the Delta, but I wanted my lures to precisely match the hatch.

By the time I left for the Big Easy, I had an arsenal of new baits. I designed the main one, the Mann's Stone Jig: 3/8-ounce, green-pumpkin, with orange strands in the skirt and an orange pumpkin grub trailer. After the Classic win it officially became known as the Delta Special, but at the time, it didn't even have a name. I brought another anonymous bait with me, a dark purple, red-flecked plastic paddle tail worm now called Swim Worm. The other key bait was a Super Finesse Worm (a weightless soft plastic). These specialized lures weren't available for the general public. The only guy throwing them was yours truly.

Buckling Down

The final practice in the Heart was short but very sweet, and I finished with about a dozen bites. So during that two and a half hour ride to the fake weigh-in, I can't say my gloom was snapped, but I did realize it was time to get serious, because I had a legitimate shot. When it was over, I still planned to quit, but I was creeping ever so slowly into the zone. There's a day in between the last practice and the start of the tournament. The three nights before it I'd been getting drunk on Bourbon Street. Not tonight. I could have gotten away with partying, but instead I ate room service in my hotel and looked over my maps. It was on.

I'm Not Dead Yet, People!

You could survey a thousand people, and besides my family, Pete, and a few close friends, I bet nobody knew that I was on my way out. They probably still don't. In public, at meetings, Autograph Day, or the zillion events happening during the Classic, I was having fun and joking around, because I didn't want to let my fans down by moping around, and I didn't want to make a formal statement announcing my plans. I'd just fish this tournament and ease out the back door. When my sponsor contracts were up, I'd quietly let them expire. When BASS sent the entry forms for the next season, I'd quietly decline the invitations. Mike Iaconelli would make news as quietly as possible. Go figure.

When I showed up to Media Day, where anglers sit at tables giving reporters interview opportunities, it turned out I couldn't have told

DETECTIVE WORK

When I catch a fish, I analyze it. Sick as this sounds, the first thing I do is look down its gullet. Often, stuff sticks out of their mouths, so I'll grab my pliers and yank it out. It might be a fish tail, frog's leg, or crawfish claw. Ninety percent of the time, everything comes out dead, but sometimes that meal is still fresh enough to maintain its color. Sometimes it's so fresh that it's even alive! I caught a bass once, and before I even glanced in its mouth, a little shad popped out and flipped around on the deck. (I treat any passengers as catch and release, too, of course.) Honestly, the process is really sickening, but it's a small price to pay to find out what the fish have been eating for dinner.

If there's nothing in that bass's throat, you can also feel the belly to determine what they're eating, a method I learned during my old Top Rod Bassmasters days. If the belly is squishy, they probably ate a soft grade fish, like a minnow or a shad. When it feels crunchy, they've most likely gulped crawfish and are having trouble digesting the shell. And if you sense an object turning end over end, say hello to the spine of a blue gill. When I tell people about rubbing bass love handles, they look at me like I'm a fish molester. Well, mimicking the forage is key. "Match the Hatch" is a golden rule of bass fishing. For that kind of insight, I can handle looking a little perverted.

anyone even if I'd wanted to. At every other Classic, even as a rookie in '99, the press hovered around my table the entire day. But in '03, hardly anybody bothered to stop by. I sat by myself almost the whole time, thinking, "People! I've got the potential to win. I've got stuff I want to talk about! This might be my last tournament!" It made me feel like walking away wouldn't make a dent in the fishing world, anyway. Maybe they wrote me off because I headed into the Classic after a solid but unspectacular tour season. Plus, I'd already clinched my spot through the 2002 Northern Open way back in October, so I didn't need to fish the last four events of the season, which meant I was off a lot of people's radars by June. Whatever the reason, I decided to use it as motivation. I told myself, "Nobody wants to talk to me? Fine! I'll give them plenty to talk about tomorrow!"

26 MY CLASSIC BEGINS

Day One

The minute my trio of alarms blared, I was more excited than I had been in months. On the first day of the Classic, between the opening day jitters and all the fans and reporters getting up in your grill, there are a million distractions that can potentially scramble your brain. But I found my focus right away. I was barely watching the road as I drove to the official launch site at Bayou Segnette State Park. Instead, I visualized every twist and turn of my ride through the Gulf of Mexico to the Heart. (But let's be honest, that wasn't just about getting in the zone. I needed to make sure I knew this long, out-of-the-way route backward and forward. After all, one wrong turn, and I'd end up in Cuba!)

DON'T WASTE ANY TIME

During the Classic, there's usually a reporter or an ESPN camera guy riding along in your boat. In the past, I'd always been matched up with high-profile media types. Not this year. My only passenger was an observer, just some dude from Louisiana who was a local club and Federation angler. He had two jobs: make sure I wasn't cheating, and transmit each catch back to BASS on shore. "First keeper in at 8:01 A.M. Fifteen inches long," and blah, blah, blah.

When I reached the Heart, as usual there was nobody else around. The silence surrounding me was so sharp, it was almost deafening. I started with the Stone Jig, scented with a little MegaStrike for good measure. When I was close enough to the mouth, I threw my first cast of the 2003 Classic. The bait barely hit the water, when boom! Jig gets eaten! Crack! Set the hook. A 2¼-pounder right off the bat!

Did that just happen?

I didn't scream, yell, or "go Ike." Honestly, I was too shocked. My local dude scrambled to get the catch entered on his little computer thing, while I threw my second cast to the same spot. Crack! Another one! Then another, and another, and another! I'd caught a limit in only five casts! Nothing like that had ever happened to me! I had ten pounds in my live well in less time than it takes to boil pasta. That was the start of a completely insane day where I racked up thirty keepers. Thirty! It could have been more, but I lost and missed a few! Think I'm lying? Call BASS, it's all logged. I went into culling overdrive. My observer practically had a spasm, and his fingers were on fire trying to report the data back to shore! He just kept saying over and over, "You're gonna win this tournament!" I mean seriously, what are the odds of catching thirty fish on the first day of the Bassmaster Classic without another angler around for miles?

THE ART OF CULLING

Tournament rules state you can only have five fish in your
live well at one time. Once you've caught that five-fish limit,
if you catch another it's time to stop fishing and make a
decision. A fish needs to be set free. It's a predicament every
angler wants, but how do you go about eighty-sixing the
runt, without wasting too much time or accidentally picking
a heavier fish? Keep in mind, some bass may be shorter
but heavier, others longer and thinner. Sometimes the differences are slight, maybe an ounce or two, but a wrong decision can mean lost spots in the standings, lost points in the
yearly standings, or even worse, a lost tournament. It's not
unusual for the winning margin to be only a few ounces . . .
and you'll kick yourself if you threw that weight back into
the lake.

For a long time, I used to weigh out fish with digital
scales. It was effective, but took lots of time to be precise. I
had to compare sets of fish against each other, and it was
easy to mix them up, since the fish often look identical. So I
looked for something better, and switched to the technique I
use now, the float system. If I catch a big one, maybe three
pounds plus, he's probably not going anywhere, so I just put
him in the well, as is. But I'll tag anything smaller with a
color-coded float, a pin that goes in his mouth, before tossing him in the well. Different colors are designated for
different weights. White means less than a pound, pink
equals a pound, yellow is a pound and a half, etc. Let's pretend I have two in the well that I know are big, plus three
color-coded ones. The next big bass I catch, I identify the
smallest color-coded one by the tag, and toss it back. If it's

hard to tell between the two lightest fish, I hang them from both sides of a beam, which are like hanging scales. Gravity never lies. The heavier fish goes down, the small fry goes up, and then goes swimming. This system is fast and effective, saving me valuable time on the water, and minimizing the risk of throwing away a heavier fish. It's culling made into a science.

SHOULD I STAY OR SHOULD I GO NOW?

I eventually had a critical decision to make. One approach would have been to leave after about ten keepers and twelve pounds. That would have been a good start, and I'd save a few for later in the tournament. The other theory, the one I used, is when they bite, you don't stop. I'd spend all day in the Heart and catch as much weight as possible. I had two big reasons.

One: I was in tidal water. I knew that the first couple hours of Day One would be the best tides of the tournament, with the super low water levels that I really wanted. Every day after, I knew the tides would push the water level higher and higher, which would toughen the fishing. When the tide is perfect, like it was that first morning, it's a big-time feeding opportunity for the bass. I had to exploit it while it lasted.

Two: I didn't know what tomorrow would bring. Southern fish tend to be sensitive to weather changes, and can shut down pretty easily. What if the conditions turned cold tomorrow? If I could catch twenty pounds that day, I was gonna take my twenty pounds. If I needed to hook one hundred fish to do it, fine. I risked smoking them out for the rest of the tournament and drying up the spot. But hey, a fish in the hand is worth two in the bush, or something like that. So I fished the Heart until the very last minute of fishing time had passed, and left with around 15½ pounds in my live well.

Day One Weigh-in

The weigh-in starts with anglers sitting in their boats, which were lined up waiting to enter the New Orleans Arena while smoke and fireworks entertained the crowd. It's all one big sewing circle. "Haven't heard anything about him," or "That's a good weight for today," and "I heard his bag is fat." The most common weights tossed around in the backstage gossip were between eight and ten pounds, with a couple of elevens and twelves tossed in. I felt good, because I knew I was above that.

Finally, it was my turn to step onstage. Just like in baseball, where a guy can choose the song playing when he comes to bat, we can choose the music playing in the arena when we enter to weigh in. Most guys play typical country and western tunes, which are fine, but not my style, to say the very least. Some guys show a little taste—Gerald Swindle and Ish go with hip-hop, and Kevin uses some heavy metal—but good music isn't the norm. Since I consider myself more evolved musically than the rest of the guys on tour, it was important that my choice took it up a notch. With that in mind, I decided to kick it old school the first day, treating the crowd to Run-D.M.C.'s "Down with the King!"

The bass was bumping as I approached the scale and Fish Fishburn, BASS's resident MC, announced my weight: fifteen pounds, six ounces! I'm sitting in first! Around twenty guys hadn't weighed yet, but I was leading the pack. Even after waking up at 4 A.M., using every stitch of energy to make a thousand casts, and waiting forever in line, my adrenaline was flowing. Good thing, too, since Fish wasn't quite done with me yet.

My Solo Battle

BASS may not want me to spill this, but whatever. As I was getting shunned by most of the press during Media Day, Fish sat down at my table and said BASS wanted me to breakdance during the weigh-in.

Excuse me? That seemed bizarre, even to a former member of the Unique Rockers. My first thought was "No way!" I wasn't about to make a spectacle of myself without a good reason. We debated back and forth, but then struck a deal. Getting time to plug our sponsors during weigh-ins was like pulling teeth. I told Fish for an extra five or ten minutes, I'd kick it old-school onstage. He agreed, but I didn't think much about it. I wasn't even sure if he was serious.

He was. After my bag was weighed, Fish looked at me and yelled, "We hear you have a little side talent!" The speakers blasted "Supersonic," the old J.J. Fad song, and then I looked to the side of the stage and saw they already had the cardboard laid out for me. It was too late to back out.

My moves were killer! I started pivoting on my hands with my legs flaring out and my feet doing some crazy steps (what we call "flair into footwork"), then got up, repositioned myself, and jumped into chino hops. Basically, you lie on your belly with your elbows against your abdomen, then balance yourself on your hands and hop around in a circle. Not easy to do. After two rounds of chino hops, I moved in for my finale, pulling out some airbornes (aka windmills). In the Unique Rockers era, I used to punctuate windmills by grabbing my crotch, but I opted to leave that out this time. And there it was. Definitely the first time a Classic weigh-in featured chino hops. History had been made.

Before that, the only dancing the Classic had seen was with Skeet back in '98, when the Dance King from California also busted moves during a weigh-in. But his were more along the lines of Chippendale-style gyrating. The issue of who the Bassmaster Classic's breakthrough dancer was has caused a little bit of controversy, since Skeet claims he was the originator, "often imitated, never duplicated." But that's a little skewed. Was he the first to dance at the Classic? Technically, yeah. But here's the difference. My breakdancing was good. I don't know what kind of dancing he was doing, although if he was looking for someone to slip a ten-dollar bill down his pants, he was on the right track.

Looking back on it, I don't know where I found the energy. I had nothing left in the tank at that point, running on pure adrenaline and the rush. When I finally saw the tape, I realized I was just going through the motions, because my face was pretty blank. That was perfect, though, because it matched a lot of faces in the crowd. Just like with anything I've ever done, there were a lot of mixed reactions. While a lot of people enjoyed it, there were a lot of confused and angry faces among the thousands of people in the house. They were looking at me, thinking, "What'd you do that for?" One look I saw a lot was shock, as in shock that I could even do it in the first place. Anglers don't generally spin on their hands, you know?

People always say the breakdancing was all part of some master plan of self-promotion. I think that's funny for two reasons. First, I actually did it to promote my sponsors, not myself. Second, Fish (and therefore BASS) asked me to do it! Still, it did get me a ton attention and strengthened my fan base among a much younger audience. At the time, the potential for positive effects didn't cross my mind, but I owe Fish!

Falling a Notch

After the weigh-in, I was whisked to a media session. I'd gotten the press's attention, just as I vowed to do. The media guys were blown away by the reports of my thirty keepers. "Does that paper say thirty? You didn't really catch thirty keepers today? Seriously . . . *thirty*?" A lot of them thought it was a misprint. Honestly, I could barely believe it myself. It was such a big number that a rumor later spread on the Internet that I hired locals to stockpile the Heart for an entire month before the Classic. What baloney! Nobody from BASS ever accused me of anything, and it's not like I took flak like that day with Dewey and the polygraph. I'm sure it was just some guy who doesn't like me talking up a chat room, repeating what he'd heard in a bar, or just making stuff up. (It's probably the same jackass who said I got DQ'ed on purpose on the second day of the '04 Classic in Charlotte 2004, or that Ish, one of my

WHAT YOU DON'T KNOW
THAT WE DO

I've spilled the beans about the breakdancing, and even butterfly collecting, so I might as well come clean on a few other
things. Maybe more than any other sport, fishing is about tall
tales and traditions. But that doesn't mean every story on the
market is worth believing. In order to get the straightest of dirt,
you still gotta be on the inside. Here are a few of the secrets
only the pros know (until now!).

1. *There is no magic bullet.* People watch pros lug huge
bags up to the weigh-in, wondering what covert, "pros only"
lure, color, rod, line, or scent we used. Everyone always wants to
know our secret. Well, here's the honest to God truth . . . there
isn't one. We're using exactly the same equipment the average
angler uses, except with ten times the confidence, knowledge,
and skill. The only secret we have? Take time to practice, then
read and research bodies of water and bass behavior. That's it.
If you come across anything telling you differently (usually with
a healthy price tag attached), take a pass.

2. *Photos are almost always staged.* This may disap-
point some people, but about 90 percent of fishing publication and Web site pictures are staged, like *E! True Hollywood
Story* reenactments. The *Bassmaster* cover photo of me
screaming after I caught the Classic-winning fish in the
Delta? Taken the next morning nowhere near where I actually
caught it, while I fought a ferocious hangover from the previous night's celebration. "How to" articles are even worse. A
pro might be doing a piece on fall crankbait fishing, head out
on the water, and not catch a thing. Well, that article still

needs pictures. Solution? Grab a fish out of the live well, stick a crankbait in his mouth, and click away. That's just the way of the world. Sorry.

3. *The truth isn't always out there.* Ninety-nine percent of pros won't tell you exactly what they used to catch their fish. They'll all tell the truth about the pattern, conditions, approach, and strategy (a big change from twenty years ago, when if pros were asked what they were throwing, they'd probably deny they even *went* fishing). But that specific lure they were using? No way. In a post-tourney write-up a few years ago, a top pro talked about cranking shallow brush while using a fall pattern. Totally honest. But then he said he caught those fish with Strike King crankbaits. Wrong! He used Bagleys and Bomber crankbaits. I was there. All pros, myself included, tell white lies because we're paid to promote certain products. But there is a silver lining. We'll often work with sponsors to develop the kind of lure we *said* we caught them on, so that next time we might not have to lie.

4. *We're not as rich as you think we are.* Many people don't understand that bass fishing isn't baseball or basketball. I'm lucky and grateful to be as financially successful as almost anyone on tour, but Kevin Garnett and I don't exactly shop together, you know? The majority of the guys on tour are scraping by, existing year-to-year, even tournament-to-tournament, often while paying most or even all expenses out of pocket. If you see a sponsor's patch, it may just be for a discount on equipment, not a giant check. Many boat sponsorships require an angler to pay off the boat when the season's over. My point? Fishing's a rough lifestyle, and only a lucky few ever get rich.

5. *Alcohol is a serious problem on tour.* **I'm not saying an overwhelming percentage of anglers are alcoholics or anything like that, but booze is everywhere on tour. Call it fishing's dirty little secret. I've never seen or heard of anyone competing drunk during a tournament, but off the water it's a different story, especially after guys miss cuts. When you're walking to room 10 in your hotel, and seven of nine rooms you pass have bottles sitting on the bureau, that's a problem. I'm not trying to embarrass anyone, just to show how draining the road can be, and to encourage anglers to take better care of each other. Groups like the Fellowship of Christian Anglers provide support to guys who want it, but for everyone else, it's often a rough go.**

best friends on tour, and I once got into a huge fight on the water. What a moron!)

After I weathered the media barrage, I hit the waiting room and watched the rest of the weigh-in on TV. Before I knew it, Mark Menendez stepped up and plunked down a massive catch of sixteen pounds and ten ounces to take the lead and bump me to second. He even got the big fish of the day. But I wasn't worried about the standings. I was too busy thinking about all those bass waiting for me. Mark didn't catch thirty keepers and have over forty bites today. Let him have first place on Day One. There was a lot of fishing left, and I couldn't wait to get back out tomorrow and catch them all over again.

AS IF I DIDN'T HAVE ENOUGH TO WORRY ABOUT

There was one thing I *was* sweating. On the first day, there was no boat traffic on me at all. But sitting in second place, I knew spectator boats— local guys on the water in their personal rides—would be following me. Fans watched us launch in New Orleans, then they'd drive down to Venice and wait for the guy they wanted to watch to drive past so they could follow him. It's actually really flattering. These guys can choose anyone they want to watch in the biggest tournament on Earth, and they're choosing me. How often can a guy get that close to his heroes? It's an amazing honor. But as much as I love having the fans close by and cheering me on, spectator boats can cause problems. The Heart was an incredibly sensitive, self-contained environment. If boats followed me in there, were they gonna stay in there and fish after I left? Will they muddy up the water? I didn't know what they'd do, and it was a horrible feeling.

When I ran into Kevin in the elevator that afternoon, my nervousness turned into full-blown fear. He started out pumping me up about my chances to win. "Mike, you've got a sweet population of fish there. Just go out there and stay steady. Catch your five the next couple days!" Hearing that kind of encouragement from a guy of Kevin's stature was awesome, until . . . "Just be careful of spectator boats. If they follow you in there, make sure they keep their distance!"

Thanks, Kevin. Now I'll sleep easy.

HOW TO WATCH A BASS FISHING TOURNAMENT

Watching from spectator boats is a great way to learn and observe things you might not see on TV. But as fishing grows and attracts more attention, occasionally we encounter fans that just don't understand the etiquette. They'll churn up water with their trolling motor, or spook fish by running outboards. It's almost never intentional, but unfortunately, it really hurts the fishing. And if we're not catching anything, there's nothing to see, right? So here are a few tips to help enjoy the action without *becoming* the action, if you catch my drift.

DISTANCE. This is the big one. A lot of times we're not keyed in on one tiny point. Wait to gauge where we're going, then keep well outside of casting distance. Considering how far pros can hurl a lure, it might be fifty or even a hundred yards, depending on the environment. Invest in a pair of quality binoculars. The polarized models are pricey, but you can practically see through walls with them.

ELECTRONICS. When you're out in the water, everything you do affects the environment. Running a simple depth finder adds more transmission noise or sonar signals. Multiply that by thirty, forty, even fifty boats, and the bass practically need earplugs. So shut off your depth finders, flashers, console, and LCD, and keep the fish less spooked.

LEAVE OUR WATER ALONE. When I work my way around a point, I usually intend to make another pass coming back. Don't assume we're done with a spot until you see us pull up our trolling motor and head off. And when we're gone, you shouldn't start fishing the area. Usually, we're planning on coming back later that day or the next. We often use this "milk run" style to let the fish rest a while before hitting the spot again. Mark the location on your GPS, and come back after the tournament's over.

BE ENTHUSIASTIC. After I catch a big one, whenever I hear the fans go crazy, the rush makes me want to catch an even bigger bass next time. The more excited the anglers are, the better a show you're likely to get. Don't be shy! Let it loose out there!

27 DAY TWO

Excuse Me While I Step Inside a Phone Booth

Remember that little problem I had with the media ignoring me? On Day Two, that wasn't an issue. All eyes were on me from the moment I arrived at the dock. The whole scene was surreal, capped by the strangest thing of all. Deion Sanders, who was there doing work for ESPN, interviewed me. Deion Sanders! I don't know if I was more freaked out about meeting Deion or the pressure of the second day. Turns out Neon Deion is an avid fisherman, and surprisingly knowledgeable. He asked how I felt about my chances. When I told him I thought they were good, he said he saw in my eyes that I was pumped and in the zone, the way athletes understand each other. We finished up, and I thought, "Whoa! *Primetime* just interviewed me! That's strange," but it wasn't enough to throw my concentration.

It also wasn't enough to distract me from my paranoia about the spectator boats. As much as I had wanted the notice before, the attention from the fans and media was only making my anxiety worse, and I think it pushed me over the edge. I became determined to throw off the crowd, so I borrowed a totally obnoxious, bright orange Banana Republic T-shirt from Pete and threw on a camouflage Dick's Sporting Goods hat that I knew would stand out. I made sure fans and media saw me in this ridiculous outfit during the launch, so they'd look for those clothes to recognize me as my boat passed Venice Marina. But once we launched and idled out to where we got up on pad, I threw on my regular tournament shirt and sweatshirt. I basically pulled a Clark Kent, even peeling the assigned numbers off my windshield, so none of the fans could identify my boat. How's that for paranoia!

ON SECOND THOUGHT, SOMEONE FOLLOW ME!

Before we took off, I told the chase boat driver, a local who was driving the camera guy assigned to me that day, that I was heading to Delta Duck, and gave him my route. He said, "I know a lot shorter way." Well, I had my directions on GPS and wasn't about to stray from them, so we agreed to meet down there. At the time, I didn't think anything of it. What did I care how the chase boat got there?

Well, I should have, because that decision to split up became one of my defining moments of the Classic. I was halfway through my trip, running full speed into the Gulf of Mexico, knifing through huge waves at 70 mph, when the motor on my boat cut out. Done! I was dead in the water. I looked around and saw nothing but open water, with only an occasional oil rig or platform breaking up the horizon. I was sitting there in a panic, turning the key, and getting no juice. It was horrible.

Normally I would have screamed and started kicking stuff around the deck. But for some reason, I didn't. Instead, I very calmly opened up the engine casing, made sure the wires were connected, then opened up the battery hatch to see if the battery terminals were on. I'm no

MacGyver, but I know enough to give a battery the eye over. But the engine still didn't start.

I lay down on the deck for maybe thirty seconds, taking deep breaths. My whole season, Classic, career, and life were flashing before my eyes while I drifted aimlessly in the Gulf. But I didn't let that frustration wash over me. I sat up and continued making calm, logical decisions. I called Trip Weldon, the tournament director, on my cell phone and told him to send me a replacement boat. Of course, if I just made my chase boat follow me, I could have swapped boats and been on my way. But I couldn't waste time kicking myself. I had another call to make, this time to Chad Smith, one of Yamaha's pit crew guys, to see if there was anything I could do to fix the problem, assuming the motor wasn't totally blown. He took me through a checklist. "Check the spark plugs?" Yeah. "The battery cable walls?" Yep. The tenth or eleventh thing down the list was a switch in the engine that can burn out, but it can be bypassed by disconnecting the wires. Before I knew it, the engine kicked over.

"Okay, Chad! What should I do?"

"You're good, Mike! Go ahead and run it."

When all was said and done, I lost forty minutes of fishing. But my attitude totally changed. I didn't have time to watch my back like a guy on the lam. I was only worried about having enough time to catch a limit. Every boat in Louisiana could have tailed me for all I cared.

LEMONADE OUT OF LEMONS

When I finally reached the Heart, the tide had definitely gotten higher, meaning the fish weren't biting like before. But thankfully, I was able to get into the zone fast, and used the TV guys to motivate me. The cameras were on me, and I knew I had to come through. As I drifted into the mouth, I looked right into the ESPN lens and said, "Look. This is where I caught five in a row." I threw my first cast . . . worked it real slow . . .

nothing! Let's try it again. Second cast. Crack! A 2½-pounder! Like I said, I usually do my best work with an audience.

They weren't biting on the Stone Jig, so I switched to the prototype plastic worm. I was in a time crunch, and felt like that lure gave me a better shot at catching pure numbers. I didn't have the luxury of fishing just for weight. The result was eleven keepers in two hours, twenty minutes. It wasn't what I had hoped for when I woke up that morning, but after all the drama, I was happy to survive. I had lost the forty minutes of the lowest water level of the day. If I had that time back, I really think I could have brought home another fifteen-plus pounds and blown the lid off the tournament, but that's all speculation. I honestly don't know. I never had a chance to find out.

Day Two Weigh-in

After Mark's haul on Day One, I really thought I'd need fifteen pounds a day to win. I knew I only had eleven or twelve pounds in my well, so I spent that two-and-a-half-hour drive back to the weigh-in hoping I'd linger around the Top 5 and stay in the hunt. Back in the weigh-in line, the gossip started again—"he's got this, he's got that"—but I kept reminding myself, "Screw it. I'm lucky to have what I have. Hell, I'm lucky not to be a castaway in the Gulf of Mexico!"

But here's the surprising thing. Mark destroyed the Delta on the first day, but couldn't keep it up on Day Two and took a huge drop in the standings. Then, with "Supersonic" bumping in honor of yesterday's dance, I had my turn at the scale. When I topped out at eleven pounds, ten ounces for a two-day total of twenty-seven pounds, it actually moved me into the lead! On a day I just wanted to stay competitive, I had taken the lead! I couldn't believe it!

I had almost three pounds on Davy Hite, who had moved into second after bringing in nearly fourteen pounds. Gary Klein was only an ounce behind Davy in third. The rest of the leader board read like a who's who of bass fishing. Harold Allen, Mark Menendez, Timmy Horton, and Jay Yelas were all in the Top 10. The big dogs were barking at my heels, only a few pounds off. But I wasn't worried about them. My head was still spinning about being in first. It was all so surreal, I couldn't worry about anyone else.

Going into the last day of the tournament, I was physically and mentally exhausted. I had broken down in the Gulf. My personal life was down the toilet. I was leading the biggest bass fishing tournament on the planet. But despite all that, during the second night I was overcome by this eerie sense of calm. I wasn't nervous or jacked up like I was going into Day Two. I thought, "If it happens, it happens." That was the real difference between the first and second nights. People ask me all the time, "How did you sleep? Were you nervous?" The truth is, I slept like a rock, and needed all three of my alarm clocks, plus the wakeup call, to get me out of bed the next morning.

28 NEVER GIVE UP

Day Three

My morning at the boat ramp started with the same media barrage, but mentally I was in great shape. I wasn't worrying about the uncontrollables. I knew my strategy was good. I knew my skills were good. But I couldn't control the weather or tides. All I could do was fish. If it was meant to be, I'd go down there and win it. The ESPN camera guy was on me again, along with the same chase boat driver that had left me the day before. He had gotten a twenty-minute lecture from Trip about staying on my butt, and I reminded him a few times for good measure. The dude wasn't leaving my sight until we got there. We launched onto super-smooth, calm water on Day Three. Instead of taking two and a half hours to reach the Heart, it only took two hours and twenty minutes, saving me ten minutes that would come in very handy at the end of the day. Already I felt like everything was falling into place.

FIGHTING FOR EVERY POUND

I'd beaten on the Heart's small population of fish for two days, pulled forty-one keepers, and had missed another twenty or so. But the biggest factor were the tides, which kept rising as I'd feared. I figured out that the fish were getting shallower, getting up on the flat, and into those drains that led back to the canals. I threw about a dozen casts before getting a bite. That told me right away that Day Three would be a dog-fight. I'd have to grind for every pound until the very end.

I had basically given up on the Stone Jig, instead almost exclusively throwing that paddletail worm I had used yesterday. But just as I had changed my lure strategy the day before, on Day Three I added a new element: a follow-up bait. With the paddletail, you cast out and swim it straight back, with the tail gurgling and vibrating. (When Mann's began producing the lure, we actually named it a "swim worm.") Today, the fish were swirling at the worm, but not eating it. After two days of getting smoked hard, they had gotten a little picky. But even though they weren't swallowing the bait, hitting it gave away their location. My eight rods included a spinning rod rigged with light line and the weightless Super Finesse Worm. Each time I'd get a hit on the paddletail, I threw the Super Finesse Worm back to the same spot, tempting the bass with something new. Nine times out of ten, I'd hook it. Follow-up fishing is a subtle, finesse technique that I used, even though I don't thrive on finesse fishing. But that's what the situation called for. Like I always try to do, I was fishing the moment.

Fate, Baby!

There were fifty-two competitors in the 2003 Classic, each allowed eight rods: 8 x 52 = 416. I found out later that of those 416 rods, I was the only guy carrying a spinning rod. It made sense, since most people would never bring light line and a spinning rod to finesse fish the Delta. It's a place to power fish, flip, pitch, and throw heavy or braided line. Honestly,

I never thought I'd use mine, and even debated not bringing it. It seemed illogical . . . but I just kept thinking, "What if it gets super tough, and I need to throw tiny weightless plastics?" I just couldn't get that scenario out of my head, so I brought it. I figured it'd be the rod equivilent to the panic box of lures I always carry for the toughest times. I always say things happen for a reason. Day Three just confirmed it for me.

STICKING TO MY GUNS

The fast and furious pace I had established on the first two days was now a thing of the past. It took me almost an hour to catch my first limit, which weighed only eight pounds. All I could do was chip away bit by bit, working the water until I finally had about twelve keepers, including two good ones, two decent ones, and a scrawny twelve-incher. At the very least, I needed to be able to dump that midget fish. But time kept slipping away. It was the bottom of the ninth, two outs, and I wasn't getting any bites. I had to make another critical decision.

During the practice period a few months back, I caught a few in a little pocket off the main channel near Venice Marina. It wasn't a winning area, but I tucked it away as a spot to save for an emergency. With ten pounds max in my live well and only about twenty minutes to score a winning weight, I was staring an emergency in the face. If I left the Heart that second, I had time for a quick pass through that emergency area. I hadn't touched it in over a month, much less fished it dry. It wouldn't have been a stupid decision. But my heart told me to stick it out and live or die by my magic spot. I was gonna work the Heart until the bitter end.

To add color to the footage they're shooting, the ESPN camera guys love to get the anglers talking. The guy on me knew what was going on, and what was at stake. With about ten minutes left, my cameraman said, "Mike, real quick, I want you to analyze your day, and tell me what you're thinking." I broke everything down, recapping how tough my day was, and how proud of myself I was for working so hard. I told him I wasn't quitting, that I'd fish up until the very end, that it wasn't over yet. As if on cue, I cast that paddletail, and one came up and boiled on it. My eyes lit up, and a split second later I had that paddletail reeled in. I grabbed the spinning rod and threw the Super Finesse right into the center of the rippling rings. Thousand one . . . thousand two . . . The bass shot up and sucked in the bait! I set the hook, and the battle that has become an ESPN staple highlight was on.

GET YOUR SCALY BODY IN MY BOAT!

This fish put up a serious fight. He wanted no part of my live well. In reality, the whole thing took maybe thirty seconds. But to me, it was an eternity, like one of those movies where everything goes . . . in . . . slow . . . motion. I was pulling in a 3½-pound fish on light line with a spinning rod. If I screwed up my retrieve even a little or the line snagged on a submerged branch or vegetation, it would snap and the fish would be lost. But I knew that was the winning fish, and that I had to get it in my boat no matter what! Finally, I drew the fish in, lay down on my side, and pulled him on board. I held him up and screamed my head off. "Never give up! Never give up, man!"

Fans always say, "That was the winning fish! Why didn't you put it in the live well immediately? Weren't you worried about losing him?" Let me explain something. I had the Grip of Death on that sucker, where a fisherman holds that son of a bitch by the mouth, good and lipped, and his hands turn into pliers. Unless someone hacked my arm off, that fish was going nowhere. You couldn't have pried it out of my hand with a crowbar. Once that fish was on the boat, it was mine.

When my little outburst was finished, I settled down, strapped in all my rods, and double-timed it back. I yelled to my chase guy, "Stay on me! Don't you dare leave the back of my boat! I was white-knuckling the steering wheel the whole way, scared of running a sandbar, blowing the engine, or God knows what else that could have ruined my catch/win. I didn't relax until I reached the ramp.

IKE'S BEST CATCHES

Fishing fans have seen highlights of me catching the winning fish at the 2003 Classic in the Louisiana Delta. That will probably go down as the most important fish I've ever caught. But it's not the only one with a special place in my memory bank. Take a look at some of my other favorite catches. What's surprising? None came during official competition . . . and they weren't even all bass!

1. *"The One."* Caught at the Poconos with the bait I stole from Pop, it was the first bass I ever caught. It wasn't the biggest or most explosive strike, it wasn't the toughest fight I've ever had. But it hooked me on bass fishing. Without it, I might be writing commercial jingles right now (or more accurately, getting coffee for the guy writing them) instead of fishing for a living. Hardly a substitute, I'd say.

2. *Almonesson Lake, NJ (1990).* I had just graduated high school, and doing a ton of local fishing on my first sea craft, a tiny polyurethane Coleman Crawdad johnboat, straight off the shelf. One battery, one trolling motor, and that's it. No extra weight. While I was retrieving my crankbait, I accidently snagged a huge fish. After five cranks, I knew two things: it wasn't a bass, and I had no control of where it was going. So it literally pulled me around the lake like a horse-drawn carriage for fifteen minutes! Finally, it tired out and I was able to scoop it into the boat with two hands. It was a gargantuan carp, at least four feet long and forty pounds, hooked through the dorsal fin. This was the first monster fight I'd ever had. Junk fish or not, that was one of the most memorable moments I've had on the water.

3. *Santee Cooper Lakes, S.C. (1997 South Carolina Invitational).* During the first official day of practice, I was jigging a spoon in the deeper sections of the lake. After giving it a couple pops and jerking the lure up off the bottom, I felt such a huge tug I actually thought my line was snagged. Turned out it was a monster ten-pound, one-ounce bass! For a long time, that was the biggest fish I ever caught. I couldn't believe it! Unfortunately, when the tournament started, I had visions of that big fish dancing in my head. I was still green enough (stupid enough, really) to ditch any backup plans and put all my eggs in that deepwater spoon pattern. I ended up crapping out in the tournament. Moral of the story? Don't let practice—no matter how good—completely dictate what you do during competition. But even though it screwed me, I still loved that fish!

4. *Lay Lake, AL, Bassmaster Classic (2002).* At the official pre-practice in June, I was flipping boat docks down near the dam and *whack!* That fish was on hard and just bulldogged me all over the place. I actually had to trail it using my trolling motor, because otherwise, he would have unspooled all the line off my reel. I knew it wasn't a bass, but who cares? The fight's always fun, no matter what kind of fish it is. It turned out to be a big, ugly flathead catfish, forty-plus pounds. Forty pounds on a bass fishing jig! That's good stuff! It's not the only time I've had to follow a fish, either. At the 2004 Arkansas CITGO Bassmaster Elite 50 (one of the four events of the new series BASS created in '04 and is expanding in '05, they're also known as E-50's) I hooked a nine-pound bass on six-pound test. If I had pulled hard on it, my line would have snapped. So I followed it on the trolling motor, like a dog owner follows a puppy on a leash until it finally tires out.

5. *Lake Seminole, FL (Georgia Pro Open—2002).* **My biggest bass in the States, a ten-pound, thirteen-ounce sea monster, and I couldn't tell anybody, or even "go Ike." Why? I got it during the practice round, and any celebration—let alone one of mine—would have let most of Florida know where the fish were. Can you imagine how hard it was to keep something like** *that* **under wraps? That thing was every angler's fantasy! I drove around all day with that beast in my live well, unable to part with it, until it finally got dark and I had to begrudgingly let it go.**

6. *Senaruco River, Venezuela (2003).* **I was in South America for the CITGO Classic Adventure, a made-for-TV tournament that pit me against Gerald Swindle, Skeet Reese, and Kevin VanDam for nothing but bragging rights. Whoever caught the biggest peacock bass was the winner. If you've never seen a peacock bass, picture a redfish, striper, or smallmouth shot up on steroids. I threw a massive twelve-inch topwater lure called a Prop Bait, and the fish hit it so hard, the splash looked like a Cadillac fell into the lake. The fight, which took twenty minutes, was harder than anything I'd felt in my life, like I'd hooked Jaws on the end of my line. The peacock weighed nearly fifteen pounds, so when I finally got it to the boat, it was too big for the net. The guide had to use a boca grip, almost like a pair of ice grips, to grab it. It's all on tape, so I can relive it whenever I want.**

7. *Cancun, Mexico (2004).* **I managed to find a week during the post-2003 Classic hubbub to go with my buddy John McGraw to Cancun for five days of sun, partying, and fishing. We got a killer deal on this Notorious B.I.G.-style yacht, complete with an entire crew to attend to our needs. We ended up**

catching amberjack, a killer game fish, in two hundred feet of water with saltwater gear. It was a huge challenge. I'm talking about hour-long fights to bring in one-hundred-pound amber-jacks, who tend to dive when hooked, to the surface. It was a to-tally amazing experience. Whether it's fly, freshwater, or saltwater, fishing always kicks butt.

29

THE MOMENT OF TRUTH

The Final Weigh-in

Back at the boat ramp, I was again waiting in line, but this time, BASS held the anglers they predicted as the top six finishers, keeping them in a group that would weigh in last. They'd been tracking information as it came in off the water, and had an idea of who had a legitimate shot at winning. It was Gary Klein, Davy Hite, Harold Allen, Jeff Reynolds, Kenyon Hill, and me. The rumor mill was still going strong, with one nugget in particular catching my attention: Gary Klein supposedly caught a fourteen- to fifteen-pound sack. If Gary had that weight, I knew I'd be taking second, end of story. Deep down inside, I still believed I had enough weight to take the tournament. But I wouldn't know anything until I weighed in, and waiting around to hit the scales was like Chinese Water Torture.

DOWN TO THE WIRE

To add some drama, they pulled us out into the arena in reverse order of our projected finish, from six down to one, with fog, smoke, lights, and pyrotechnics going off everywhere. Pure rock and roll, baby! One by one, they brought us up to be weighed. Whoever held first place would take his spot in the "hot seat" while guys tried to knock him off. It's an incredibly tense situation for the guys on stage and their fans in the crowd. Eventually, it came down to me and Gary, who weighed in first, and boy, did his bag look huge! But when he put those fish on the scale, all I saw was what number he didn't hit—15 pounds, which I knew would beat me. The little digital numbers had stopped at 11-14. As Gary took his spot on the hot seat, I started breathing again, knowing that at about 9½ pounds behind, I had a shot to catch him.

THE MOMENT OF TRUTH

With Eminem's "Lose Yourself" blasting through the arena, I stepped up to challenge Gary. But as I grabbed my fish from the live well, Fish stopped me. "Wait, before you take them, we want to show you this highlight." Up on the Jumbotron, they showed the highlight of me hauling in that last fish. It was crazy! It had only happened a couple hours before, and now I was watching myself scream, "Never give up! Never give up!" on a massive screen. The crowd went wild. The whole thing was insane!

Finally, the hoopla ended and I began the walk I've been dreaming about since I was old enough to hold a rod. My heart was pounding through my chest. Slowly the bass trickled out of my bag and onto the scale. They flopped around, refusing to settle long enough to get an accurate weight. The numbers steadily crept up, tick by tick, until they hit . . . ten pounds, fourteen ounces! 10-14! I had beaten Gary by just over a pound and a half.

Mike Iaconelli, the freaky, tattooed angler from South Jersey, was the 2003 Bassmaster Classic champion!

The Champ Is Here! The Champ Is Here!

The second they announced the number, I completely and totally freaked out. I couldn't believe it. I'm gonna be in the record books, with legends like Rick Clunn, Larry Nixon, and Denny Brauer? I've reached the point most anglers never get to? Wow, dude! I'm the Bassmaster Classic champ!

Streamers and confetti rained down as 2002's champion, Jay Yelas, came over and handed me the trophy, along with ownership of a title he'd cherished for a year. As usual, Jay was the epitome of class, quickly telling me "good job," then backing away and giving me my moment. I thanked him. As Jay passed the mantle, so to speak, Fish whispered in my ear, "Hold it over your head!" I had no idea how heavy that trophy would be, until I hoisted all fifty-six pounds of it in the air. I felt like a power lifter. As the trophy went up, its metal and polished wood shining in the lights, I looked down—and this is wild—the first people I saw were my uncle, mom, and grandmom. And right away, I felt Pop's spirit. It couldn't have played out any better. I saw their pride, happiness, and joy. They'd worked so hard and supported me for so long, helping me to achieve my goals. I never would have made it without them. It was a pretty awesome moment.

The Victory Lap

I went back inside my boat and was taken on a victory lap around the arena. Now that was cool! Eminem was cranking. I was waving the American flag and holding the trophy over my head. It's something I'll never forget. I was milking every ounce of the joy, yelling and screaming like a maniac at anyone I knew. I spotted John McGraw, my best friend, who'd promised that if I had a shot at winning, he'd fly down for the last day, and he did. Friends like that are rare, you know? He was screaming, and pointed at me with a "Woooooo!" It was money!

Best of all, I rode with my mom beside me. I don't think that's ever been done. Most of the time, the winner's wife rides shotgun. But I had my mom, and that was even better. She hates attention, and I imagine she was a little reluctant to climb aboard, but the BASS people probably ushered her over without giving her a chance to say no. I'm sure she thought the spotlight should just be on me, but it wouldn't have been the same without her, you know what I mean? Then I called Drew and Rylie. They were so excited, screaming "Daddy won! Daddy won!" Even Kristi congratulated me before putting the girls on the phone, which I appreciated. Everything about the moment was perfect.

MIKE'S DREAM FIVE

The Louisiana Delta may be the site of my biggest win, but it's not my favorite fishery. It takes so much to make a lake truly great. A wide variety of species. Variable environments, from heavily covered shallow flats to deep verticals and open water. A touch of scenery never hurts either. Unfortunately, those qualities rarely determine how BASS and FLW choose tournament spots. If a town has a lake, motels, and enough cash to get either tour's attention, a tournament will be scheduled there. But if BASS or FLW named me emperor (scary thought, I know!), these are the lakes I'd put on the schedule. Call it my "dream circuit."

1. *Lake Champlain, New York/Vermont.* Often called "the Missing Great Lake," this massive fishery is tops in the country, hands down, and among the world's best, too. Its combination of world-class fishing and spectacular environment can't be beat. I particularly love how the northern end combines vertical, rocky drops with flat, weedy water. On trips with Top

Rod Bassmasters, we'd stay at Gwen's Cabins on North Hero Island, where the species diversity makes it an angler's Shangri-la. If you caught a hundred fish, twenty-five might be largemouth bass, twenty-five trout, twenty pickerel, ten walleye, ten crappie, and ten perch. All in a picture-postcard setting. Add my history (my first major win in '99 was here), and there's nowhere on the planet I'd rather fish.

2. *Lake Guntersville, Alabama.* Out in the boonies, Guntersville's no resort town. But if you want to go crazy on largemouth bass, that's your spot. There may be nowhere better for size and numbers. The key is the grass, specifically the thick milfoil and hydrilla lining the lake bottom, allowing the fish to thrive and grow. My first time there was for the 2002 Alabama Tour Pro, and it just blew me away. Fishing Guntersville is like dying and going to largemouth heaven!

3. *Lake Okeechobee, Florida.* One of the country's biggest freshwater lakes, Okeechobee's a huge, beautiful hole in the middle of Florida. Part of its appeal is the history. It's the Yankee Stadium of bass fisheries. I grew up captivated by tales of Florida guys like Roland Martin catching eleven-pounders in the cattails. The first time I pulled out of the marina into the main lake, I was awestruck. No land in sight. Like Guntersville, Okeechobee is known for its grass, but instead of hydrilla and milfoil, which are submerged, it features emergent species. Those reeds, cattails, and lily pads create an amazing visual, while harboring the big bass Florida is famous for.

4. *Lake of the Woods, Ontario, Canada.* Hundreds of miles of undeveloped shoreline, untouched water, and protected wilderness, in perhaps the most spectacular environment I've ever seen. Imagine fishing with grizzly bears hunting along the shore and bald eagles flying overhead. The water holds perhaps seventy species, but most visiting anglers fish walleye and pike. That means bass waters are virgin territory, so the fish, even by fish standards, are really stupid. They've never seen artificial lures. It's a long bus ride getting somewhere that remote, sometimes even a float plane trip. Once you're there, ask around for "Big Joe," a mammoth dude, maybe seven feet and three hundred pounds. He's one of the best guides I've ever met and will do you right, I promise.

5. *Alloway Lake, New Jersey (R.I.P.).* The best lake in New Jersey, possibly the entire Northeast (aside from Champlain, of course), Alloway was a private lake Top Rod Bassmasters had access to through one of its residents and where I really cut my teeth. It was small, only three hundred acres, but had grass, wood, rock, deep and shallow water, plus every species of fish imaginable. It was your classic South Jersey lake: formed by a creek draining into the Delaware River that was dammed in the eighteen hundreds to provide power for the mills. Eventually the dam needed repair and the state offered to fix it if the homeowners put in a public ramp and opened up the lake. They refused, so the state drained it. I cried when I saw it afterward. That was an angling tragedy. Thankfully, those greedy Alloway Homeowners Association idiots shot themselves in the butt. When that lake was gone, so was their property value.

Honorable Mention: Delaware River (New Jersey and Pennsylvania). It's not the greatest fishery in the world, but I grew up on its banks. You gotta give your home water props!

IT'S JUST GETTING STARTED!

From there, it was non-stop madness. I was whisked from the victory lap into a media conference, doing interview after interview after interview. It's hard to believe these were the same guys ignoring me four days ago. They had plenty to say to me now. Then I got shuttled to the Classic Outdoors Show across from the Superdome, into a sea of fans at the Yamaha-Ranger boat display, all wanting autographs and offering congratulations. After that, it was the victory banquet, swapping stories with a bunch of former champions and industry bigwigs. I had the kings of the fishing world fawning over me. This was better than I could have ever dreamed!

By the time the banquet ended, I'd been up since 4 A.M., going non-stop at full throttle until around 9 that night. Well, guess what? I didn't even need my second wind. First words out of my mouth? "We're going to Bourbon Street!"

30 LET'S GET CRAZY . . .

Animal House!

My crew for the night included Pete, John, and our buddy from Portland, Travis Kline. We barhopped up and down Bourbon Street, eventually hitting a bar where basically the entire fishing industry was drinking and partying. Gerald Swindle. Byron Velvick. Kevin. Skeet. Ish. Anglers. Sponsors. Everybody! People getting crazy, rowdy, and drunk . . . and nobody more than me! It was just nuts. Everybody was buying me drinks, and I was doing shots, pounding beer, guzzling Hurricanes, you name it. Then this MC called my drunken self out on the dance floor to do some breakin'. Somebody, probably Ish or Skeet, told the DJ to play "Planet Rock." I took my shirt off, so the tats were in full effect while I did my thing. It was all just a silly, crazy celebration.

When Dance Party U.S.A. ended, I put my shirt back on and went to the bar, my radar locked on this hot blonde. She was from Alabama, in town by pure coincidence, but she knew fishing and we totally hit it off. Before I know it, we're on our way to her room at the Ritz-Carlton. It doesn't get any better than that. Not only had I won the Classic and landed a smokin' hot chick, but her hotel was an upgrade over mine! That's the kind of night it was—just sick!

I'm Ready for My Closeup . . . Not!

When my new friend from Alabama and I got to the Ritz, it was 4 A.M. I had to meet the BASS photography staff in *my* hotel lobby in three hours for a shoot. Needless to say, we didn't sleep a wink. The next morning back at the Marriott, as everyone was waiting for me to come down the elevator, I strolled in through the front door and smiled. "Hey guys, I'll be right down. Let me just go put my tournament shirt on." I'd been rolling on no sleep for twenty-six hours, and guess what? I wasn't tired! Pure adrenaline! We drove out to the boatyard to do a bunch of promotional shots for ads, magazine photos, even a *Bassmaster* cover. Either I photograph really well, or they broke out the airbrush, because those pics turned out pretty good. Especially considering I was drunk as a skunk in every one.

Letting It Sink In

After my drunken photo shoot was over, I finally got back to my hotel room for a couple hours of sleep. You should have seen the place. Travis was sprawled out on the floor, John was in one bed, and Pete in the other. Everybody was still hungover and half drunk. We were like a bunch of frat guys on spring break. Four freakin' dudes shacked up in one room, living like scobos with socks and dirty underwear scattered all over the place. And in the middle of it all was an elegant Bassmaster Classic champion's trophy sitting on the bureau. It was the funniest sight! I wish I had pictures.

Sitting in that hotel room and drifting off to sleep, the reality of what I'd accomplished started sinking in, and I began to reconsider the decisions I'd made before the tournament. I told myself, "Everything, my breakup, my pain, my depression, and now my win, happened for a reason." And that's when I knew the truth, and allowed my brain to understand what my heart and soul knew all along. I couldn't leave fishing. Not now. Not while I have this amazing opportunity that I never had before, and may never have again. I couldn't walk away from it. I went to sleep knowing I was still a fisherman.

GOOD EATIN'

That night, as a thank you to the people who had supported me, I got my family, Pete, John, Travis, and a few more close friends, together for a killer steak dinner at Smith and Wollensky in New Orleans. Pete called ahead and told them the Bassmaster Classic champion was coming, so they had the prime room ready in the back, with glass walls overlooking the entire restaurant. It was the most amazing dinner I ever had. Everyone was in a great mood, laughing and having a great time. I had the best steak on the menu, an incredible fillet. I had never paid a dinner bill over a thousand dollars before. It was worth every penny.

A Classic Champ's Work Is Never Done

After the tournament, I had to hang around for three more days to do more media stuff. The first and last days were pretty standard—just the same interview over and over. Where'd you catch them? What did you use? How do you feel now that it's over? But the middle day was . . . interesting. I flew to Little Rock for a day's worth of studio work at J.M. Productions, Jerry McKinnis's studio that is responsible for most of ESPN's BASS programming. Now I don't necessarily want to label what happened that day as a "groupie" thing, but I had just won the Classic and made that new friend from Alabama. So in Little Rock, a young chick shows up at the studio. A smoking hot intern at JM Associates who had made a point to be there that day, even though she didn't have to be. After I finished in the studio, she volunteered to drive me back to my hotel in Little Rock, and . . . see it.

This was getting weird. Up to this point, my groupies had always been forty- or fifty-year-old southern white men. All of a sudden, hot chicks started coming out of the woodwork. I guess being a Classic champ has its perks.

What If?

So if I had finished second, would I still be fishing? Honestly, I don't think so. I'll say this, if I had had a mediocre finish, like my thirty-eighth in 2002 on Lay Lake in Birmingham, I guarantee I'd have been done. But once I held that trophy over my head and experienced the moments afterward with my family and friends, I remembered my true passion for the sport. I loved it too much to leave. It's my life.

So once again, I had to give notice at Dick's.

31 HEADING BACK TO JERSEY

i The Road to Revolution

I already knew that I wasn't quitting by the time I left New Orleans, but all the possibilities this win provided truly started kicking in after Pete, John, and I did that long drive home. That's when the wheels started spinning. I talked to Pete, John, even out loud to myself, trying to figure out where to go from here. I was so consumed by the opportunities, that out of those twenty-one hours on the road, I only slept for maybe three. Of course, when the Bassmaster Classic trophy is seatbelted in the back-seat, it tends to keep you focused on the task at hand.

I Get By with a Little Help from My Friends

Pete and John sticking around for that drive back meant so much, be-cause they provided two unique and totally great spins on the situation.

It felt like we were philosophizing around the campfire as we wrote down idea after idea on a tablet of yellow notebook paper. The first five hours, the pad was just a mess of thoughts. After ten hours, those thoughts became a physical outline. By hour eighteen, we had a very organized, structured concept of what we believed I needed to do. What's amazing is that we did all this while my cell phone was ringing off the hook with media requests. Apparently, BASS had given out my number. I must have done twenty-five interviews on the ride home.

ASKING THE OLD KINGS

One of the first things on the menu was contacting former Classic champions we had good relationships with. Jay Yelas, one of the nicest, straight shooting guys on the planet, was a natural choice. Afterward, I called Dion Hibdon and Kevin. We intentionally asked each guy the same questions, to get an idea of things that worked well for each, along with strategies that failed. I probably talked to each for about an hour.

I bombarded them with every question I could imagine. How would my sponsorships be affected? What media outlets did they use to promote themselves? What should I expect as a daily rate for seminars and workshops? At the time, I was asking $500 per day, which I thought was great. When Jay told me the rate should jump to two or three thousand a day, my jaw hit the floor. If I hadn't had this discussion, I would have gotten pimped by promoters. Kevin stressed how my value would increase, but that all anglers should be making more, and as Champ I was in a unique position to help it happen. I needed to make sure I demanded my true value. That was a breakthrough moment, recognizing the degree that anglers have been absolutely exploited by sponsors and the industry, and knowing someone else was trying to get what was fair. Dion focused on time management. I'd get tons of opportunities, and couldn't stretch myself too thin. "You could do a million things to increase your value, Mike, but if you crap out on the water next year, what's that mean?" In other words, stay competitive!

Just like I did on my assignments at Rowan, I wanted to give this project a theme—something that would summarize our approach. The word we came up with was *untraditional.* From that single word, we developed a concise, aggressive business plan . . . a plan that worked way outside the box.

UNTRADITIONAL THROUGH AND THROUGH

For an untraditional business plan to work in my world, it has to reach untraditional people. People who'd never heard about fishing. Suburban kids. The elderly. Everyone and anyone. The average Joe doesn't read *Bassmaster* magazine and *BASS Times*. You have to reach them through the daily papers, television shows, and magazines that have traditionally ignored fishing. That was the future. But getting into those media outlets would be tricky, so we decided I needed a publicist. Nobody had ever hired one winning the Classic, but to us, it seemed like a no-brainer.

Another key was reaching untraditional, nonendemic sponsors, the direction we knew the sport needed to head anyway. Money in the fishing industry is tapped out. There's no room for growth. But companies outside fishing, like Pepsi, Nike, or Rolex? That's where the cash is. Some guys had tried reaching those nonendemics, but I don't think anyone had ever approached it concentrating as heavily on the means as the end result. Kevin, for example, had his eyes on the prize, but it's like he was trying to leap frog over the necessary steps, like increasing his broad-based appeal as an athlete. We were trying to create a blueprint to reach the pot of gold at the end of the rainbow, which in my mind was the huge, nonendemic sponsorship. I was one of the first guys who recognized that those results couldn't logically take place without first being well marketed and getting your name outside the fishing community.

Everything I learned at Rowan started creeping back out. I thought, "Wow! So that's why I learned that." People assume I picked my major because of fishing, and congratulate me for thinking ahead. In reality, it just kind of happened. I try to tell people that back then, I assumed I'd be writing copy for an ad company, but they just smile and shrug it off. "Yeah, right."

Infamy's Softer Side

Pete focused his input purely on the business side, the dollars and cents. He's always handled that part of the industry better, anyway, so his insight was key. But John took a more humanitarian spin. "You've got this excellent platform, Mike. Don't piss it away. You need to do something besides just make money." That really lit a fire under me and inspired my involvement with the V Foundation. This organization, named after Jim Valvano, NC State's legendary basketball coach who fought valiantly but ultimately succumbed to cancer, has raised over forty million dollars for cancer research. I decided to create Anglers Pounding Out Cures, a program where I donate two dollars for every pound of bass I catch to the V Foundation. Fans can match my catch with a pledge of their own, or simply make a donation. Having been touched by this disease on a personal level, I wanted to do my part to help find a cure.

But beyond just helping people because it's the right thing to do, charity work could help the sport itself. One of the big problems we face is outsiders who think we're not professional athletes, just a bunch of bubbas fishing with live bait and drinking beer. All big-time sports like the NBA or NFL have a strong charitable presence, so it's not only worthwhile, but also legitimizes our sport. It helps show, "Look, we *are* professional athletes. We do the same things they do." These are the kinds of things we need to do if we want fishing to be the next NASCAR, blowing up on the American sports scene. Maybe we won't get there, but we have to try.

PLAYING THE GAME

I've also tried to follow the lead of guys like Denny who are doing things right. Aside from the smooth and charismatic way he presents himself, I noticed some of the more subtle things Denny does, like making himself an ally of the tournament organizations. He'd help out BASS with commercials, membership drives, or appearances, often for small or even no dollars. But those things help the sport, which in turn helps him. Denny's a master promoter and showed me it's occasionally okay to give your value away, as long as you're in control of that decision.

I wasn't the first angler to establish strong relationships with BASS or FLW after a big win. But only a week after New Orleans, I was at the FLW Championships talking business with Irwin Jacobs himself. A week later, I was in BASS headquarters in Montgomery for a staff meeting. No champ had ever tried to use his new status so quickly. I'm just glad Helen and Dewey weren't running the show anymore. Officials so resistant to change wouldn't have played ball with me at all. Not sincerely, at least. Kevin dealt with the same anti-Yankee stuff when he first came on the scene. Then he started winning and the old regime tried to use him like a northern pawn, purely to milk money for themselves and their organization. Today's powers that be use me, too. I know they see me as a guy who can promote the sport and make them money. But at least Irwin, ESPN, and BASS milk me with fishing's best interests in mind. That's a difference I can live with.

I don't worry about looking like a kiss-up, either. Skeet always says that I put on a show for every camera, but it's not about brownnosing. There are two reasons I don't want to be an enemy of the state. First, a strong relationship with the organizations means they'll consider you for the opportunities they provide. I'm not stupid. I know how the game works, and that sometimes you have to play ball. I'd be shooting myself in the foot, both in advancing my career and the sport, if I didn't compromise a little. And in return the tours have never said, "Pose naked and stand on one foot," or anything that would put me in the position of having to say "No way!" Second, because I've established solid relationships with BASS and FLW, I feel comfortable voicing my opinion when they do things that I think are bad for the sport. Hopefully, people understand my true intent is to increase fishing's television exposure and get more kids involved. I'm not interested in being *anyone's* patsy.

32 MOVING FORWARD

Biting the Hands That Feed Me

I worry that as the sport grows, the anglers are being left at the bottom. The tour organizations and the athletes have to grow together. We need to be part of the decision making process. We don't want to control or own the process. But we need to have more input into what goes on in our careers, our livelihoods. Right now, we have the PAA to help us voice our concerns, but until anglers really band together to form a solid, cohesive unit where we put our collective interests before individual agendas, we won't get everything we deserve. Years of miscommunication have built distrust from a lot of anglers toward BASS and FLW. Look at what's happened in baseball, basketball, and hockey, when management and the athletes can't stay on the same page and the games stop. It's the fans that suffer. I don't ever want to see a day when we boycott tournaments. Nobody wants that. But as a group, anglers have

some gripes, and we need to find some common ground with the tour organizations, and make sure our voices are heard.

And our concerns have been addressed in the past. A great example
came back in 2001, when BASS proposed to change how Classic berths
are divided up among anglers. Under the new plan, they drastically reduced the number of spots that came from the tours, leaving us with
only half. This was a huge deal, and we freaked. The tours are our majors, where the elite anglers fish. They should set aside half as a starting
point, then work their way up! They also planned to do bizarre things
like automatically include the past two Classic winners and Anglers of
the Year. Huh? I don't expect to make the 2005 Classic because I won in
2003. Sorry, it's all about "what have you done for me lately?" After the
Angler Advisory Board spread the word, we had informal PAA meetings
where we talked about boycotting. We made a lot of noise, and BASS listened, stopping the plan in its tracks. That was great, because it not
only showed our voices could be heard, but also that despite our periodic
differences, anglers can still come together when we need to.

Just Gimme the Boat!

Those were nice examples of where things got fixed. But other problems
are still out there. One biggie on both FLW and BASS is that during the
last two tournament days, the cut days, we're forced to drive the
Purolator Boat, the Fuji Film boat, the Everstart Boat, or some other
wrapped tour-sponsor boat, instead of our own. That kills us when we
try to attract new sponsors, because it takes away a major bargaining
chip—a boat fully wrapped in that sponsor's logo, with prime coverage
in front of the cameras. That's a serious selling point we're losing out
on. Plus, boats are part of our equipment, as important as lures and
rods, and we're forced to fish without our own. The PGA wouldn't ask
Tiger Woods to play the weekend without his own clubs. NASCAR
wouldn't make Jeff Gordon drive somebody else's car. Why should we?

The tournament organizations would say they use those exclusive sponsor contracts to increase prize money, which benefits us. And that may be true, but in the long run, does it help us more than hurt? I'm not always sure.

Sharing the Wealth

Do I think the organizations pass along their income to us as well as they could? Now there's a loaded question. Let's put it this way: there's room for improvement. FLW does it better than BASS. Their prize money is better and pays farther down the standings. But even then, it's only barely getting to where it needs to be at the top and the bottom of the prize money ladder. We're getting the short end of the stick at both. Yes, BASS and FLW are businesses that need money to run their tours, but I can't believe, in an era where they've got million-dollar sponsorship contracts, that my thirty-ninth-place finish on Lake Eufaula in '04's Alabama Bassmaster Pro netted me only $2,700. That's ridiculous! It can cost $3,600 just to enter the big-time pro tournaments. Thirty-ninth out of more than 150 anglers, and I'm not breaking even? That hurts the legitimacy of our sport. In tennis and golf, thirty-ninth place on the money list means at least a decent living. In fishing, thirty-ninth means a third mortgage and debt to your eyeballs, unless you can make it up through sponsorships. That's not as easy as it sounds. Again, it comes down to anglers being too low on the tours' list of priorities. On a list of ten, we're seventh, tops. I've never seen a detailed analysis of BASS's or FLW's financials. I'd love for them to open up the books, and prove me wrong, that they're doing the best by us that they can. If I'm off base, I'll be the first to admit it. But I doubt that's the case.

But FLW, despite filtering down more money to us, has its own drawbacks. While BASS allows us to wear whatever hat and shirt you want on cut days, FLW makes you wear their shirt with their sponsors. I'm lucky, since I have crossover sponsors in Ranger Boats and Yamaha. But an angler sponsored by non–FLW-affiliated companies is forced to sign logos of companies that don't pay him, or even worse, might be in direct competition with companies that do! Just like with the boats, taking away our shirts and hats kills our sponsorship opportunities. Again, middle ground is necessary. Maybe we'll wear an FLW sponsor's primary shirt, but get to represent our sponsors with small patches. Something! With Wal-Mart behind them, FLW can use shelf space in stores to leverage potential sponsors, especially nonendemics, to play ball. I know it happens, too. There has to be a way to compromise on the issue, to make everyone happy. It starts with getting anglers and tournament directors in a room to talk. That just hasn't happened yet.

A Positive Note

I've just said a lot of negative things about the organizations, to illustrate that there's a need for anglers to come together to represent our interests as a group. But all in all, the positives with BASS and FLW are so much greater than the negative. I feel that both tours are 100 percent committed to advancing the sport and remain genuinely passionate about it. As long as they don't lose that, I honestly believe these other problems can be worked out.

33 SPONSORSHIP

Brother, Can You Spare a Dime?

When you're a club fisherman, sponsorship is the Holy Grail. It's beaten into our brains that when you're sponsored, you're in the club and learn the secret handshake. It's what every angler trying to make it to the next level wants. When I first looked into sponsorship while fishing at the Invitational level, I was starting from scratch. I had no idea what to do. The first thing I found was a very general monthly sponsorship newsletter. I compared its information to what I read in other magazines and what I heard from other anglers. What I realized is that getting sponsorship was like getting any other job. You have to show a company you can offer something they can use. In fishing, what they need you to do is push products. That matters as much, if not more, than your actual talent. If you can move a company's stuff, you've got a shot. That's the first concept aspiring anglers have to understand.

I started out by sending out a very basic resume to around twenty-five different companies whose products I liked. When you're not sponsored by anybody, you pursue everybody because you need everything. Rods, reels, lures, trolling motors, clothing, boats. I'd even solicit competing companies like Strike King Lures and Zoom Lures, since I wasn't aligned with anybody. Of those twenty-five inquiries, I didn't get a single yes. Only five or so even bothered to say no in writing. The rest just tossed my application straight into the trash.

SCHOOL'S IN

As I was learning how the game worked, I attended a Bassmaster University Class (talk about coming full circle, I teach them now). One of my teachers that day was Guido Hibdon, who I fished with in '94 when I won the pro-am on Lake Norman. After the seminars and lectures were over, I waited patiently for a chance to talk to him. Not only did he remember me, he talked to me for fifteen minutes, giving me all kinds of advice about sponsorship. I know now how busy pros can get, and Guido could have easily blown me off or cut our time together short. Instead, he took time out to teach me. That was incredible, and something I always try to do with students in my seminars.

Small-time Negotiations

Nothing makes you more appealing to sponsors than success. Back in '97 and '98, I was gaining notoriety from winning a lot of tournaments in the Northeast. I started to understand the sponsorship game, too, and before too long, I had signed standard, one-year contracts with my first sponsors, Mann's Bait Company and Fenwick Rods. I became part of Mann's Elite Team, one or two guys picked from each state to help move product in their region. So I was finally rolling in corporate dough, right? Hardly! In a contract typical for many anglers, sometimes even those with solid resumes, all I got was a limited amount of free product and discounts on everything else. But I had sponsors, so even though both deals meant squat, financially, I could legitimately wear a patch on my vest. That was huge!

A Little More Love from Mann's

It wasn't until after the '99 Classic that I started generating actual income from sponsorship. I had a better understanding of what it meant to promote, sell, and market. I also started realizing the strengths of being from a different demographic and standing out from the pack. But it's not like I woke up one night in a cold sweat and said, "I need to establish the Mike Iaconelli brand right now!" It all built up slowly, in the stairstep process I always preach.

My first real negotiations were with Mann's Bait Company in '99. My puny product contract was up, putting me in limbo. In the meantime, right before the Classic, a competitor, Bandit Lures, came to me with a *very* small financial deal. And I do mean *very*. But it was cash! It felt like real, true sponsorship. With my win at the Federation Nationals, my qualification for the Classic and the tours the following year, I felt I had some leverage to try and negotiate a better deal from Mann's. I barely knew jack about jack, but I'd try anyway. I figured Bandit had lowballed me with their offer (Rowan had taught me a few basics, after all), but still only guesstimated my value by using Bandit's offer as a starting point. And according to the people at Bandit, I was worth a minuscule hundred or so dollars a month. Pretty sorry, huh? In the end, Ike the Master Negotiator managed to pry a couple hundred a month from Mann's, and I stuck with them. I felt like Donald Trump! During those stages, I always took the low road. When they said that's all they could give me, I took it. I didn't know my value, and the process was intimidating. I was used to negotiating nightly rates as a DJ. Selling myself in this industry was something new.

What I eventually learned was that most beginning sponsorships, even for more established pros, generally are only between one thousand and two thousand dollars a year. At the semi-pro level, making more than five thousand dollars in sponsorship would be awesome, but that barely touches the huge costs of entry fees, travel, lodging, airfare, gear, and food. If you happen to be a family man, throw in your mortgage, wife, and kids. Five grand ain't really doing much for you, huh?

I'M THE MAN, MANN'S!

My successful rookie season in '99 bumped my value even higher, and I got a taste of another part of the business. As my newly renegotiated contract with Mann's was ready to expire, I was approached this time by a headhunter hired to create a pro staff for a lure company called PRADCO, a conglomerate of smaller companies like Bomber Lures, Cotton and Cordell, and Arborgast. He offered me one thousand dollars a month. That was big money! Just as before, another offer helped make my value more clear. Again, I took that offer back to Mann's, and thankfully, they were able to stay competitive.

I kept returning to Mann's because they'd always treated me well, and loyalty is important to me. I've been with the same lure, boat, line, and rod companies for a long time. But at the same time, it's business, and I work hard to get my fair value while maintaining good relationships. One way to do that is with back door incentives. When I enter into a contract now, I'll take a smaller amount on good faith, but stack the contract with incentive bonuses. A Top 5 finish equals bonus money. Qualifying for a Classic, bonus. Winning a Classic? Bigger bonus. Instead of signing a contract for four free appearance days, I'll agree to one, and anything else comes at an added price. This way, companies can make a smaller initial investment, but I get compensated better for success. And when I do well, their logos are all over the place. Everyone's happy.

I also love designing products, the big example being the Stone Jig, which I had the opportunity to put into mass production. That makes royalties super important. PRADCO was willing to make the Stone Jig, but didn't want to pay me for it. Mann's gave me royalties at eighteen cents a jig. It turned into a great deal for everyone when after my Classic win the Stone Jig went from a Northeastern phenomenon to a huge national seller. Pradco eventually came out with its own jig, which bombed. I still laugh about that. So it's not always the base number of a sponsorship that matters. I try to be creative with sponsors to find ways to make everyone happy.

Another way I do that is to start with a company whose product I love, and offer them a year at below market value. In exchange, I tell them that when I'm successful, at renegotiation time I'll be asking for much bigger money. For example, I've loved Team Daiwa products since my Poconos days. Even when I signed on with Fenwick, I was still using Daiwa in the shadows. So after I had some leverage and choices for rod sponsors, I left other offers on the table, went to Daiwa, and offered to work a year for only product. That may sound like I was moving backward, but it wasn't. I really felt comfortable with Daiwa's product, and my ability to succeed on the water and make it pay off. Did it work? Absolutely. Daiwa's now a very lucrative sponsor.

LEAVING IT UNWRAPPED

Negotiations can get hairy. I ran a wrapped Kellogg's boat for a year, and was running Yamaha when I won the Classic. But I wasn't making much doing it, which I felt was ridiculous. A wrapped boat is a huge value I shouldn't give away. So I decided to leave my boat unwrapped until I got a better deal. At this stage of my career, I had an obligation to myself— and the sport—not to get shortchanged. I'd cost myself money in the short run, but hopefully with long-term success. Higher risk, higher reward.

My boat and motor contracts expired after the 2004 regular season, but I still had BASS's inaugural E-50 season to fish. I was forced to borrow boats from friends, who all know I drive them rough and insisted on getting theirs back in one piece. I had to be more cautious, so I couldn't hit those spots the other guys won't, which is one of my strengths. I even had to fish one tournament from a jet boat, which tops out at 40 mph. No wonder the E-50's were forgettable for me.

But there were benefits beyond exercising my principles. I was having discussions with some of their competitors, and Ranger and Yamaha may not have taken our renegotiations as seriously if they hadn't seen I was willing to walk. Eventually, during the last E-50 event of the '04 season, the media started asking, "How can the Classic champ not have a boat and motor sponsor?" It was embarrassing for the higher-ups at Ranger and Yamaha to get called out like that. We got a deal worked out. In the end, I didn't hit a home run playing hardball, but I didn't strike out either. And most important, I played.

My Own Jerry Maguire

It's difficult for fishermen to approach big companies with no inherent connection to the sport. That's where those untraditional media outlets come into play. I've appeared on ESPN2's *Cold Pizza* and Fox's *Best Damn Sports Show Period*. I've been featured in *Esquire, GQ, Playboy,* and *ESPN The Magazine*. These outlets give me exposure to companies outside the industry who might want to play ball, once they see fishing's potential. But we're talking big business here, deals way beyond my ability to "close." That's why I made another important hire: my sports agent. Before the Classic, Pete and I started investigating sports agencies. Ninety percent weren't interested. But one, FX Marketing out of Tampa, took a chance. Pete and I signed on with them in '02 and the bottom line was, our agent couldn't sell us. His mistake was trying to sell the sport and not the angler. After New Orleans, I gave him three months. When he still didn't produce, I fired him and started looking for new representation.

SPONSORSHIP LEVELS

Early on, when Pete first started teaching me about value, I developed three very detailed levels of sponsorship, which I present to interested companies at the start of negotiations. Each level defines what I expect financially and what companies get for their investment. It's important for anglers to take this step, even if they're young and less established. Obviously, guys without an established track record like I've got need to be realistic, but they shouldn't give themselves away for free. Here's my system.

Associate Level sponsorship: The bottom rung and my minimum sponsorship, ranging from $12,000 to $25,000. The minimum is $1,000 a month. I won't promote a company for less. Associate level sponsorship includes no free promotional days. If a sponsor wants me to appear at a sporting goods store, that's okay, but they'll have to pay my daily appearance rate of $3,000. An associate sponsor won't get a logo on my boat or truck, and only appears on the bottom half of my tournament shirt, which isn't exactly prime real estate. But if a company wants to get their feet wet with the Mike Iaconelli brand, an associate level sponsorship is a great way to do that at a minimal cost. That sponsor can use my name and likeness to promote their product, so it has benefits for them.

Key Level sponsorship: Step two, around $50,000 a year. But the added cost means added value for sponsors. Their logo appears on the top half of my jersey, and the side panel on my hat. They'll get secondary level logoing for the truck and boat, plus four free appearance days. I have four sponsors at that level. Like I said, I try to be creative and flexible. That means I might get a check for $25,000 and a free boat. Or 25 grand and a free motor. Or $20,000, plus my entry fees paid. Value comes in ways other than just a check. Remember that.

Primary sponsorship: My top sponsorship level. The big one. The logo goes in what I call "Primary Shirt" location, meaning it's an inch off the top, easily seen in photographs, and the primary panel on the front of the hat. My boat and truck will be entirely wrapped, making it the "blank, blank" boat and the "blank, blank" truck. I include eight free appearance days. This runs $100,000+ annually. And unlike the first two levels of sponsorship, I don't have this one filled yet. It's the big non-endemic I've been hunting for, where the future of fishing lies.

Luckily, Octagon, a huge agency that represents high-profile athletes like Anna Kournikova and Davis Love III, had their eye on the fishing market. I was surprised, but it makes sense when you check the numbers. In terms of participation, the sport is a monster. I'm talking twenty-eight million people across the country, more than tennis and golf combined. ESPN is involved. Plus, it's virgin land. I saw opportunity with them, and they saw one with me, so I signed with them. The key, which I hope they know, is to sell the angler, the personality, and brand, along with the sport. They need to sell Mike Iaconelli. To go back to the NASCAR example, that sport blew up when people started seeing the guys inside the cars. In fishing, it's about highlighting the anglers' personalities. That's what BASS should be doing too. They could probably work hand in hand.

34 WHAT'S HAPPENING ON THE WATER

Gentleman's Code of Fishing

During the second day of 2004's last E-50 in Paducah, Kentucky, Rick Clunn and I happened to cross paths on a spot we'd both fished the day before. At the time, Rick had a great shot at winning, and I had fallen out of contention. Without being asked, I ceded Rick that stretch of water. When the tournament was over, he thanked me for letting him have it. It was my pleasure, because I knew he'd have done the same for me. It's all part of fishing's "gentleman's code," unwritten rules stating that when there's an argument over who has a spot, the angler who's doing better as the tournament progresses should have first crack at it. It's a rule I take very seriously, because I have an enormous amount of respect for the sport and its traditions. But there's a lot of gray in this unwritten rule. If I were still in contention that day, it would have been just as much my water as his, and I probably wouldn't give an inch. Rick and I would have been fishing head to head.

Or maybe I would have. There are more times when I've left water I felt I had a right to fish than I want to remember. Each time, I've regretted giving up the spot. I remember on Lake Eufaula when I ceded a cove to Charlie Hartley that was big enough for the both of us. Not because of the code, because I had as much right to that water as Charlie, but because I was intimidated. There was no confrontation, shouting, or fighting. I just left with my tail between my legs. Yeah, I have a reputation for fishing aggressively, for not giving up water when I have a right to it. But I end up with the short end of the stick all the time, because the "gentlemen's code" is as much about gamesmanship and intimidation as it is fairness and order.

What Are You Talking About, Edwin?

There've even been times when other anglers have broken the code, and somehow I still ended up the bad guy. During Day Two of the Mississippi E-50 on the Tennessee-Tombigbee Waterway, I was working an oxbow where I'd spent nearly the entire day before when Edwin Evers entered. At the time, I was sitting in ninth place, higher than Edwin, and he should have ceded me the water. I very calmly asked if he was there yesterday. When Edwin said no, I told him I was in the Top 10, and would appreciate him giving me the water. It's something I've done a million times for other anglers, and they've done a million times for me. Not this time. Edwin went nuts, screaming that he found that oxbow in practice, that I never give anyone else respect on the water, and that he wasn't moving! Then he started railing into me about a tournament on Lake Eufaula the year before, which he had won, and I actually ceded him the winning spot! On the first day, he had cut me off to get to this pipe that was shooting out water. I knew he was jockeying for the space, so I just gave in.

Then I hit a nearby pocket, but it was too small for me and the other two boats there. So I left altogether, giving Edwin the cove, and, in a roundabout way, his victory. This was the ammo he's using? I went ballistic.

When I called him out, he immediately got flustered. "Well, I didn't mean me! I meant you didn't give Matt Reed any space." Matt Reed is Edwin's buddy from Oklahoma, who was fishing the pocket I hit after letting Edwin have that pipe. Matt Reed and I did test each other's boundaries, but we never argued about it. And even if we did, it ain't Edwin's business! So I screamed, "Edwin, you're not Matt Reed! Where's this argument going?" We had drifted to within punching distance of each other, and my blood was boiling. Thankfully, Edwin's amateur partner, who displayed monster guts by getting in between two pros, talked us into our neutral corners. Edwin left, I won that battle, and we avoided each other the rest of the tournament. But a few months later, I saw him at the 2004 Classic. We wished each other luck, and everything was fine. I don't hate Edwin and definitely respect his skills. I think he understands that. But to me, he disrespected the code. And bringing up this Matt Reed stuff was ridiculous. It shows how intense things get on the water. When your tournament life is at stake, it can get really hard to wade through the gray areas of our "code."

Clarifying the Code

I'm sure there are pros who could tell you about times I've violated that gentleman's agreement. And I'm sure, unconsciously, I have. But I honestly can say I've never purposely, knowingly gone out of my way to do it. That's just not how I fish, even though I'm out there to win. I'm aggressive, but I'm no thug. But that's the problem with an unwritten code. There's so much room for interpretation that two reasonable people can come to totally different conclusions about the same incident. We need to put our code of ethics in writing, maybe through the PAA. It won't solve everything, but it would definitely remove a lot of the guesswork from the process.

There *was* one absolutely hilarious thing that came from my run-in with Edwin. After the tournament, some non-boating little jerk must have gone online and started spreading stuff nice and thick about the confrontation. Soon, it was all over the Internet that Ish Monroe and I had a huge shouting match and threw down! Are you kidding me? Ish is a very good friend of mine and was nowhere in the vicinity at the time. Oh, one other tiny detail. Edwin's white and Ish is the only black guy on the tour! How do you mix those two up? Ish called me, laughing. "Mike, did you know we're in a fight?" We thought it was hysterical, and even joked about actually faking a fight just to throw gasoline on the fire. I'm telling you, the gossip whores in fishing never sleep!

MIKE'S PREDICTIONS FOR BASS'S FUTURE

I'm always thinking about the sport's future, and what could be done to help enhance the fan experience. I have some ideas about changes that may be in store for professional bass fishing, and sooner than you think. I don't own a crystal ball, but I'm willing to predict a couple things the tournament organizations might do . . . and I think they're good ideas.

1. *Establish a more a carnival-like atmosphere at weigh-in.* A fan would be able to show up on a Saturday morning and watch live coverage on huge screens that have been set up, almost like a drive-in movie. He'll be able to sit in the stands, eat popcorn, and watch the action on the water while waiting for the weigh-in. Every minute of action could be simulcast on shore, even dividing the screen to view different anglers. Obviously, there are technical and logistical issues to work out, but it would be an amazing experience for fans, and I think that's what you're going to see.

2. *Look for changes in the format.* Say we're fishing Santee Cooper Lakes in South Carolina. BASS would set aside a specific area like Black's Creek, and save it exclusively for the cut days. They'll divide Black's Creek into twelve holes, and guys will rotate between them. Grouping us in one place would allow fans to sit on the banks and watch their favorite angler hit a hole. If there's no bank access, spectators could watch from pontoon boats. Fans will love seeing us figure out the fish in an area we haven't seen. This format would highlight some of fishing's coolest elements. Depending on how the sun, wind, or currents change the water, some spots would be better at different parts of the day. Anglers at the top of the standings would have first choice of where they wanted to start, allowing them to time out their day and rewarding them for good work on the previous days. It would require a ton of strategy. Most important, this format is very TV friendly, and in some ways, is fishing at its purest. Anglers would head into unfamiliar territory and be forced to fish the moment, which, to me, is pure fishing. BASS and FLW may not define it that way yet, but everything changes at some point.

These changes became more likely the minute ESPN purchased BASS. They're all about growing the sport and making it viewer friendly, because they know that's the best way to draw new fans. ESPN will push the envelope, and FLW will have to follow. That brings me to my third prediction. Plotlines. Scripting alliances and rivalries. Dudes beating each other with steel chairs and largemouth bass. "Next week, Iaconelli and VanDam in a steel cage!" (Okay, I'm kidding about this one.)

35 MY YEAR AS CLASSIC CHAMP

Everything Changes

Putting that trophy over my head changed my life, from fishing to my personal life to professional opportunities. I went from being days away from quitting to fishing international competitions in Venezuela and Spain on someone else's dime. I'm casting with Deion Sanders on *The New American Sportsman.* Acting as the Grand Marshall of the Disneyland Parade. Throwing out first pitches at baseball games. Crazy stuff that I'd have never imagined doing. Even in my personal life, I was able to enjoy being single instead of agonizing about it.

John Hancocks and Souvenirs

I expected the sea of autograph requests immediately after the Classic. I did just win the world's biggest tournament. But it hasn't let up. I get fifty e-mails a month with requests for autographs, which blows my mind. It's a good feeling, knowing I've had such an impact on people. But it also feels bizarre, sometimes. I still look at this sport through a fan's perspective. It's why I try to answer my e-mail personally or stick around to sign every last autograph, even if it eats into my personal time. I always remember the extra fifteen minutes Guido Hibdon gave me. If he had blown me off, I might not have been as successful getting sponsors. Maybe I'd never have gone pro. I want to give back, too. Have I ever unintentionally blown someone off? Probably. But I've never gotten mail that said, "You jerk!" (Actually, I have. But not regarding autographs!) So that's good.

For me, the funniest stuff is seeing "Iaconelli gear" land on eBay. The boats we used in the '03 Classic were presold to local dealers. Well, the one who got my winning boat put it on eBay, and ended up getting another ten G's on top of the boat's value. I guess some dude really wanted it. I don't ever look for my stuff, though. I'm not a real eBay junkie. I just hope my underwear or something doesn't turn up. I don't think I've been that careless. As long as they haven't been signed, they'll have to take DNA samples to prove they're mine!

36

2004 BASSMASTER CLASSSIC

Preparation

There are so many demands on your time after winning the Classic that anglers often follow up with a terrible season. Not me. Despite endless media appearances, a demanding tournament schedule, and traveling the planet promoting sponsors and my sport, I went into the 2004 Classic on Lake Wylie in Charlotte on the heels of a strong season. I even had a shot at Angler of the Year going into the final weekend at Santee Cooper Lakes in South Carolina. It didn't happen (I finished third in the AOY standings), but I knew I was fishing well, and was ready to become the first repeat Classic champion since Rick Clunn back in '76 and '77.

But to repeat, I'd have to conquer a completely different fishery. Lake Wylie and the Louisiana Delta are like yin and yang. It starts with size. On the Delta's five hundred thousand fishable acres, I was able to find secret spots like the Heart, and keep boat traffic from being a big problem. Lake Wylie is only thirteen thousand acres, meaning I'd be elbow to elbow with other anglers, spectators, and weekend joyriders. Its deep, clear water is ideal for power fishing, but I knew I'd have to rely on finesse techniques if things got rough. During my pre-practice a month before the tournament, I worked two areas where I thought I could win. The main lake area, which had deeper, clearer water, and also further upriver, which was full of shallows, nooks, and crannies. I had a great pre-practice in both, but decided to stay on the main lake and focus on bigger fish and higher-quality bites. The biggest reason? That boat pressure I anticipated would affect the deeper water less. As always, I chose baits to match the hatch, settling on lures like a green pumpkin Stone Jig that imitated bluegill, and a deep-diving crankbait that resembled shad.

People ask me all the time if I called Rick Clunn for advice about how to repeat as Classic champ. I didn't, not because I don't respect Rick's opinion (he's still a hero of mine), but because I was fishing better than ever, and didn't want anyone, not even Rick Clunn, to skew my approach. I didn't solicit any advice or outside information leading up to the event.

Uh-Oh!

During the first week of July, after pre-practice ended, I was able to spend a little time back in Jersey. It was great. Not only was I able to sleep in my own bed and see my girls, I'd have an easier time stepping up my workout program like I did before the '03 Classic. On the road, all I can do is hit whatever's in the hotel fitness room or use the small set of weights I keep in my truck. That makes it hard to maintain consistent workouts. But I have a gym up the road from my condo, equipped with everything I need. The extra endurance from my added fitness was a huge advantage in the Delta, and I hoped it would help again on Lake Wylie. So I started kicking it into gear. I was a little worn down, but didn't think much of it.

Not until my second week home, that is. I was leaving the gym after just forty-five minutes of cardio, a pretty easy workout. The next thing I remember, some dude was lifting me off the ground. I had blacked out and fainted next to my truck. I landed in the hospital, where they kept me overnight and ran a million tests. In the end, the diagnosis was exhaustion and dehydration. It made sense. Ever since raising that trophy in New Orleans, I had been running nonstop doing promotions, shows, and seminars, all while putting in the hours to stay competitive on tour. Then there was the partying. Lots of Red Bull and vodka until 3 A.M. My schedule was so hectic that, in the fifty or so weeks since winning, I was home about three, and never even for seven days straight. I had been going at 110 percent for so long, I didn't realize my body was hurting, until it all caught up to me. This was a serious wakeup call. Fortunately, since Lake Wylie was smaller, there would be no two-and-a-half-hour boat rides, making it less physically demanding than in '03. I guess I picked the right year to pass out!

*H*eads Up, Rick Clunn

Showing up to the Classic as defending champion means every camera and every microphone is in your face. Instead of letting it bother me, I tried to take advantage, having grown so much more media and marketing savvy. I played to the cameras, cracking open and slamming a Red Bull (like I need more energy?). I knew representatives from Nike were at the tournament, getting a feel for the sport. I wanted them to know I was ready to play ball and blow this sport into the mainstream, so I had my tournament shirt unbuttoned, with a Nike shirt underneath. You bet that was intentional!

It's possible all the attention hurt my focus a little, but once they announced my name and it was time to get my boat rolling, I was all business. Just as in New Orleans, I spent the boat ride imagining that day, how I'm gonna fish, my casts and angles. After whipping my crankbait around the first two spots on my pattern and getting nothing, I hit my third spot and started flipping docks. *Boom!* First keeper. Nothing huge, but it was a nice start. My next spot was another point on the main lake, with rocks on the bottom. I tossed that crankbait, and *crack!* Seven and a half pounds! Huge for Wylie, and bigger than anything I'd ever caught in a Classic. I turned to the armada of fifty or so spectator boats behind me, and held up this massive fish. The noise was so huge, it sounded like the lake had blown up! Everybody was stoked. It was only eight-thirty, and I already had a Top 10 start. By the end of the day, my strategy of going after big bites had paid off. I didn't have a limit, but I pocketed a thousand dollars for the big fish of the day. Even better, I weighed in at 15-15, only three ounces behind Takahiro Omori, who became the first Japanese angler ever to lead (and later, win) a Classic. Denny, Dean Rojas, and Tommy Biffle were right behind me, but I wasn't concerned about the anglers, just the fish. After one day, my attitude went from "I can win this thing" to "I'm gonna win this again!"

Drew and Rylie Go Prime Time

The only thing cooler than heading to Charlotte as the champion was heading there with my girls. It was the first time Drew and Rylie had ever been to a Classic, and to be able to share it with them was amazing. Even more amazing was when ESPN interviewed them during the day one weigh-in. I was in the staging area of the Charlotte Coliseum and couldn't see, but their voices were loud and clear. They were totally outgoing, working the crowd like little hams. Wonder where they got that quality, right? The best part was when Drew was asked what she learns when she fishes with me.

"Mostly, it's that fishing teaches you patience."

That just killed me! It was great! I was so proud that they were comfortable in front of people, and that I could show them off. A lot of pros and fans didn't realize I even had kids, and the ones who did probably

IKE'S CRANKBAIT TIPS

Crankbaits describe any diving lure that dives and vibrates because of a lip in front, imitating the forage in the motion they produce and their color. As a power fisherman, I absolutely love fishing crankbaits. They work year round to cover huge stretches of water and elicit the ideal reaction strike. Crankbaits usually get stereotyped as bait just for warm water. But they're adaptable to almost any situation across the water column, which is amazing. A lot of anglers are intimidated by that freedom and don't maximize their potential. Let me boil it down.

THE SPECS. Crankbaits come in a huge variety of shapes, sizes and colors, so it's important to know the characteristics.

Wobble: The amount of back and forth motion a crankbait makes moving through the water. As a general rule, wide wobble crankbaits with lots of sound work well in warmer water (over 60 degrees), especially around wood cover and active fish. My favorites include Berkley Frenzy and Bagley's Diving B Series. In colder water (45 to 60 degrees), use a tight wobble crankbait like rattletraps, Rapala Shad Rap, and Cedar Shads to work lethargic fish in weedy areas.

Color: Like any lure, my color choice is based on "matching the hatch," so crankbaits get divided into three basic color schemes.

1. *SHAD IMITATING BAITS.* All types of shad, herring, minnows and shiners, with colors like pearl, white, silver, and chrome (gel flake colors).
2. *PERCH/SUNFISH BAITS.* Imitating sunfish, bluegill, perch, and red ear. Look for chartreuse blueblack, chartreuse blackback, brown, and chartreuse.

3. *CRAWFISH IMITATORS.* These use lots of brown, orange, and khaki, with black and blue mixed in.

LINE SIZE. This is a biggie. The heavier the line, the shallower the crankbait runs. Lighter line means deeper running baits. Each change in line size equals about a 1½-foot depth difference. Knowing this can determine and fine-tune your approach.

TACKLE AND EQUIPMENT. It's important your gear maximizes that crankbait. I like to use 6'6" Team Daiwa SLT Cranking Rods for close target casting, and a 7' model for long casts. Both are whippy rods with fiberglass in the blank, slow and less sensitive, delaying my hook set long enough for fish to engulf the lure. Berkley Trilene green monofilament line, with its extra stretch, further increases delay times. As for reels, I want a large capacity spool for long casting, and a medium retrieve gear ratio (like a 5.1 to 1) so I have the freedom to reel lightning quick or super slow. A superior anti-reverse system also helps avoid slap back of the reel handle.

BOUNCE THE BAIT. The most critical aspect, since at least 90 percent of my crankbait bites come after the lure hits off an object. That's what causes the fish to react. Crankbaits should deflect off something each time. If there's no structure to hit, change speeds or add a jerk or pause to your retrieve to add some action. But otherwise, bounce them off the cover. Rip them from the weeds. Use the lake bottom to change their direction. Yeah, you'll lose a few lures, but suck it up. That's the price of catching fish! The deflection rule also helps choose a lure's running depth. If you're fishing at six feet, you want that crankbait running six to seven feet. For ten feet, plan to run between ten and eleven feet, and so on.

hadn't met them. For the rest of the week, everyone—anglers, media guys, ESPN and BASS officials—stopped me about how cute they were. The only problem came that night at dinner, when I got a taste of the type of guys they'll be bringing home in ten or fifteen years. We were at Pizzeria Uno, and Jason Quinn, one of the only other tatted-out guys on tour (to go with funky bleached hair and piercings), was sitting across from us. My girls kept waving at him, shrieking, "There's Jason! There's Jason!" Drew was especially smitten. Hey, Jason's a good guy, but c'mon! I don't need my girls flirting just yet, you know?

Clunn's Record Is Safe Again

When I woke up on Day Two, I pictured having a day everyone would re-member. I should have been more specific, because while the day was memorable for everyone else, I wanted to forget it.

It started well enough. Just like the day before, I focused on larger fish. About a half hour in I had a small keeper in the well, but after that came a serious dry spell. I hit a couple of spots from before, including that point of rocks where I landed the 7½-pound lunker. Nada. All of a sudden, my watch was getting tight on my wrist as time was quickly closing in on me. When things are going well, everything on the water goes in slow motion. You feel like you've got days and days to kill. But when it's bad, everything's on fast forward. Time whips by.

Before I knew it, I only had a couple hours left to fish and still only had that one bass in my well. I tried rolling back over spots in my pri-mary and secondary patterns, fishing free over brand new docks, even fi-nesse fishing. Ditching my big fish plan, I lost the crankbaits and started drop shotting and throwing little worms. I just wanted to stay alive and keep myself in contention. No luck. Only twenty minutes left. Then fif-teen. Desperate, I made a last ditch effort to fish around the ramp near T-Bones Restaurant and try to catch some released fish. I should have just stopped in for a sandwich instead.

The DQ

That ramp was close to an off-limits area and I was fuzzy about where
the restrictions started. Instead of taking my chances and guessing, I
called Trip Weldon, BASS's tournament director, for an answer. What he
told me depends on whom you ask. I ended up fishing down a stretch of
riprap along a nearby road, then in front of the restaurant, which seemed
to follow Trip's instructions to the letter. But after I was loading the boat
onto my trailer, the Assistant Tournament Director told me I fished an
off-limits area and my catch for the day was being disqualified. "No way!
Get Trip on the phone!" Now, when Trip talked to the media about his
original instructions, he said, "Mike called me today around twelve-
thirty or so and asked me exactly where the off-limits was. I said, 'Mike,
if you're looking at T-Bones and go over to the riprap out where it meets
the lake, from there past the boat ramp behind the no-wake buoys is off-
limits.'" That sounds simple enough, except it sounded to me like the
riprap area was fine when we first talked, and that's what I told him. We
kept screaming back and forth, but I finally realized, "Who cares? I've
got one puny fish. Why am I arguing to save a pound and six ounces? I'm
dropping in the standings either way."

But here's the thing. In virtually every event we fish, off-limits areas
are marked with a visual reminder of where we can't go. Well, the
Classic is BASS's showcase. They pour tons of effort and money into it,
and they choose *this* event not to mark an off-limits area? That's beyond
stupid. But after I settled down, I realized that even though the area
should have been marked, it was ultimately my fault for not knowing
where I couldn't be. It was my responsibility. I was wrong and I could
live with it. Really, my frustration came more from not being able to figure out the fish than a mistake I made in the last fifteen minutes that
barely cost me any weight. All I wanted to do was go back to the hotel
and hang with my girls. Instead, I was shuffled off to talk to Shaw
Grigsby and Bill Clement in the ESPN booth, and highlights of me not

catching squat were played over and over ad nauseam. Meanwhile, Dean Rojas had overtaken Takahiro and things were heating up for a nail-biting third day, and all the attention was being paid to my mistake that capped a terrible day. But that's the media, you know?

Lemonade out of Lemons

I tried to put Day Two behind me and begin Day Three with a clean slate. I had barely made the cut, but as always, believed a comeback was possible. It would take about twenty-five pounds to do it, but why not? Yeah, those aren't great odds, but that's the attitude you always have to take on the water: "I can win. I will win." Seeking huge fish only, I ran to my secondary pattern up the river, and started out solidly enough. My first keeper was 4-14. A few more of those, and I'd be in business. Unfortunately, that was my only keeper, and I ended up finishing nineteenth. But even though the day ended up pretty weak, I don't regret my strategy. I needed huge weight and had to swing for the fences. Sometimes when you swing big, you miss. Silver lining? My one fish ended up the Purolator Big Bass of the day, nabbing me another thousand dollars. Also, my seven-pound Big Bass from Day 1 wound up the Big Bass for the entire tournament. That was worth two grand more. It wasn't the way I wanted to get into the record books, but it wasn't bad, either.

Ow, Ow, Ow, Ow!

Of course, I had already set the record for most physically painful day ever. About a half hour after landing my keeper, I flipped my jig into this gnarly fallen tree and the lure got stuck. I couldn't get it out. I was literally jamming the front of the boat into this tree, trying to poke the jig out. As I'm doing it, I saw these big bugs flying around. I knew there was major mayfly hatch going on, so no big deal. I just want my jig back

IKE'S EMBARRASSING MOMENTS

You know the *Wide World of Sports* "Agony of Defeat" highlight where that skier just bites it? Fishing has lots of embarrassing moments like that, too. Plenty happens that we're not exactly proud of. Fishing out of bounds during the '04 Classic was enough embarrassment for a lifetime. Unfortunately, there've been plenty more Classic Ike Faux Pas.

HOOK ACCIDENTS. A hook ends up buried in your body, and you start doing the mental math to remember your last tetanus shot. It's happened to me five times, and twice it was actually funny. The first one happened came while I was pre-fishing for an event on Lake Hartwell. I snagged a keeper using a Pop-R topwater lure with a #4 feathered treble hook, meaning there were yellow, white, and red threaded feathers tied onto a hook point. As I was pulling it out, the fish jumped and blew out the lure. I turned away, but the lure lodged into my face. Uh-oh! I'm alone, in this isolated part of the lake, and this thing wasn't coming out. I cut the line and stared into my reflection on the helmet I wear while I'm driving the boat. Sure as rain, the feath-ered treble was buried. If I got off the water and hit the hospital like any normal person, I'd lose my practice day. So I left it there, fishing the rest of the day with feathers sticking out of my face! I'd roll by docks and every resident thought I was a total freak. Who could blame them, really?

At least that accident happened on the water. My second year as a pro, I arrived super late to my hotel in Mobile for an FLW tournament on the Pascagoula River, and had to get all my gear ready in a hurry to grab some sleep. I actually finished in enough time to actually get five hours. So I sat on the bed to set my alarm clock. "Aaaaagggh!" A #2 treble hook I left on the bed went through my sweatpants and underwear and into my cheek! It felt like a bee the size of Alabama had stung me! Surgery time! I spent about forty-five minutes mooning myself in the hotel mirror, trying to get the treble hook out. Not only didn't I sleep much that night, but sitting in the boat wasn't exactly comfortable, either.

BOAT MISHAPS. There's any number of ways to ruin a bass boat, and I've found just about all of them. One favorite was during practice for an Invitational at the Catskills. I was still using the old Ranger Boat I won as an amateur in '94. I got to the ramp on a Saturday morning, ready to launch into the Hudson. About three-quarters of the way down to the water's edge, I looked in my rearview mirror and saw the boat sliding off the trailer! Before I could do anything, it crunched down on the ramp, three feet from the water. The area was packed, so everyone could watch and laugh at me . . . until they realized that I was clogging the ramp, a major breach of angling etiquette. We had to use a winch to get it off the ramp, and I ended up knocking a hole in the fiberglass on the bottom, making it useless for a couple weeks. Later, I learned my uncle, always trying to help, had sprayed the trailer bunks, the flat planks where the boat rests, with silicone spray to aid getting the boat on the trailer. Apparently, that also makes it easier to get it off, too. What a mess!

But it gets worse. During the club and Federation days, I was fishing with my Top Rod buddy Big John Milchanowski at a local Military Bass Association tournament (a step up from club tournaments) on the Upper Chesapeake Bay at the mouth of the Susquehanna River. We wanted to hit the northeast part of the river, and took a ten-minute run through a back channel that sidestepped the Chesapeake and saved us about a half hour. We ran it in the morning, no trouble, and left our sweet spot near

Havre de Grace Marina in Maryland with fifteen pounds in our live well. As we were heading up the back channel, up on pad, boat running full speed, I suddenly felt this *thump, thump, thump* from the bottom of the boat. Panicking, I came off pad, which was totally the wrong thing to do, because that put me lower on the water. The boat just stopped, sitting high and dry like a beached whale in maybe five inches of water. We couldn't move again until the tides came up, by which time we'd missed the weigh-in by a few hours. The tournament director was almost ready to send out the Coast Guard to find us. The worst part? We'd have won the tournament by five pounds!

This one might be my favorite. Back in '97, I fished an FLW Everstart tournament at Buggs Island. The week before, I'd finished fifth in a BASS event there by plowing up the Roanoke River, running sandbars to spots other people wouldn't go. It had worked great, so that became the plan. The first day was great, and the second day, I did well again. But running back on that second day, things got . . . ugly. I saw this back swirl in the river, coming almost in slow motion. "Oooooohhhhhhhhh Noooooooo!" It's a fisherman's nightmare, because those whirlpools mean something big is under the water. But there was nothing I could do. *Crash!* The boat popped out of the water, and before I even stopped, I could smell oil. Not a good sign. I took a look, and the whole lower unit of my engine was gone! Sheared off! Missing! Vanished! My amateur and I were totally alone, because nobody else had the guts to run up the Roanoke. It took hours to troll back to the ramp, then get picked up by a tournament official. That was a fun day.

These stories don't even include the line tangles, encounters with angry wasps (read on for that one), or other stupid mistakes. The moral of the story? Just because we're professionals doesn't mean we don't screw up. A lot.

so I could move on. All of a sudden, I felt this really sharp pinch on my arm. That's when it hit me.

Those weren't mayflies.

I had tossed my jig into the center of a wasp nest! Now it seemed like hundreds of the bastards were swarming around me. I was frantically stepping on my trolling motor, but the boat is pushed so far under the tree that it's stuck. By now I'd been stung three or four times. Every other word out of my mouth was a curse, and all these spectator boats were just sitting around, watching me get totally devoured! I took off my hat and started swatting. Bad move. They started stinging my head. I had two choices—either bail into the water and swim away, or start up the outboard. Well, if I swam off, I'd have to come back eventually, so I jumped in my console, jammed the motor in reverse, and got out of there. The end result was eight stings and a lot of pain. On the plus side, I learned I'm not allergic to wasp stings. After fifteen minutes, I popped some Advil, tied on another jig, and went back to catching nothing again.

Passing the Mantle

I was so excited for Takahiro when he ended up winning. You could see the enthusiasm in his eyes, because he had earned this, big-time. The dude came over from Japan knowing nobody and speaking almost no English, just to win this tournament. Nobody had worked harder to reach the top than T.O. It made me happy to pass the mantle on to him. When I approached to hand him the trophy, he bowed, half traditional Japanese, half Wayne's World "we're not worthy!" That was amazing. The crowd went nuts, too. But I shook my head, and pointed to him. T.O. was the man, not me. When I handed him the trophy, I said, "Remember this moment, it's a once-in-a-lifetime thing." He held it above his head, and the pyrotechnics started.

I wasn't champ anymore, but it was okay. Drew and Rylie seemed fine with it, too. They were running around, stuffing their pockets with as much confetti and streamers that had fallen as they could carry. Having them there made what could have been a hard day into a great one. We were presented with a huge novelty check for Big Bass of the Tournament. It was for two thousand dollars, but to the girls, it might as well have been for two million. They thought that big check was so cool. They really help put things in perspective.

Deep in My Mind

When I passed out a month before in New Jersey, I knew my body was physically tired. But it wasn't until the Classic was over that I understood how *mentally* fried I was, too. And I realized, in the deepest part of my mind, I was relieved not to have won again. I don't mean to sound like I tanked it. I did my absolute best out there. I just don't know if I could have done another year like that, running all over the world promoting my sport and my title. I'd read John McEnroe's book *You Cannot Be Serious* while I was researching different champions and their mental outlook, and he talked about subconsciously wanting to lose Wimbledon because he was so burned out. I thought that was ridiculous, until I could identify with him. If you had told me, even on that last day when I needed twenty-five pounds to win, that I actually wanted to lose, I'd have called you an idiot. But afterwards, when my mind and body finally had a couple days to reflect, I wouldn't have argued.

37 THE MEDIA

I Did What?

After the 2004 Classic ended, one by one, media members and industry types started coming up to me, whispering, "Mike, that was really smart! I would have never thought of that!" before they ran off smirking. Then the pro- and anti-Ike stuff popped up in chatrooms, media outlets, and in fishing circles. It was either, "Mike, I've got to give you credit. That was genius!" or, "Iaconelli! What an attention whore!" So what exactly did I do to get everyone all riled up?

Apparently, I fished out of bounds during Day Two *on purpose,* so I'd get tons of media attention on a day I would have otherwise unceremoniously fallen back in the standings. The idea spread faster than the bubonic plague.

I must be good at marketing myself, because I've got people thinking I'm way more clever than I actually am. They're giving me way too much credit. That rumor was totally ridiculous. I fished that area because I was a confused idiot, desperate to pad a horrible bag during the biggest tournament in the world, not because I'm an attention-starved media whore. What about Day Three? Did I intentionally get eight wasp stings just for some ink? Even suggesting I'm that calculated and cold makes me laugh. I was frantically fishing for my Classic life, plain and simple! A couple of three-pounders, and I've suddenly got a prayer that last day. Does anybody really think I'd deliberately toss away my day? I'm way too competitive for that! But most important, I have too much respect for my sport and fellow anglers to intentionally break a rule in a tournament. I just wouldn't do it. Never. Case closed.

Ike and the Media

I make no bones about my desire to promote myself as an angler. We make our money through endorsements, which go to the guys whose personality engages people. I understand the value of P.R. But my number one commitment isn't to myself, it's to fishing. That's where my loyalty lies. So when I hear things like that rumor, it pisses me off, because it means people think I'd compromise my sport's integrity to make a buck.

I know that a tatted-out, New Jersey Federation angler who prefers Run-D.M.C. to Travis Tritt grabs attention, positive and negative. I've been different all my life as a fisherman. All I can do is put myself out there, and people will think what they'll think. Sometimes, I don't care. Take the '04 Great Outdoor Games. I unknowingly did an interview with my cap a little crooked, like an old-school B-boy. The next thing I know, people were bitching on the Internet that I was trying to thug out the sport, as if one crooked cap is gonna bring 50 Cent and Jay-Z to next season's Classic. If I had known my cap was crooked, I'd probably have straightened it. Or maybe I wouldn't have. Who cares? It's a cap, people!

Other times, like when I told Tim Tucker I didn't think it was a big deal for me just to *make* the Classic every year, I've had to take my medicine.

That bothered people, mostly other anglers, and I understood why, even though I never meant it as a slam on them. I've learned since to be careful with my words. A lot of people think I'm cocky, and maybe I am. But whenever I've felt that perception going too far, I've tried to remind people of who I really am—that everything I do is motivated by my love for fishing.

Certain things have ticked me off, too. One time, I gave an interview where I jokingly compared the birth of my girls to winning the Classic, saying the victory was the only thing that came close. But it was printed like I said winning in New Orleans was *more* important than Drew and Rylie being born. That's going too far. You want to say I wear my hat like a punk, fine. That's fair game. But when somebody devalues the birth of my children, it hurts me personally. That's what makes me upset with the media.

Lots of people say that all publicity is good publicity, as long as it keeps you in the public eye. To an extent, I agree, as long as the publicity accurately reflects my personality. I guess that's where I draw the line between good and bad publicity. Perception. Everything I do is an expression of myself. I'm not putting on an act for the cameras. That's how I am. I get just as excited catching a four-pounder while fun fishing as I do during a tournament. I love to catch fish. If people want to think I'm all about hype, so be it. I can't fix that. But one thing I insist people comprehend is my respect and love for fishing. Outside of family and close friends, nothing is more important to me. Everything I do is with an eye toward making the sport more popular, this decade's NASCAR. Nobody has the sport's best intentions in mind more than me. As long as that idea is understood, I don't really care what people say about me.

Ike's Popularity Within BASS

I know I have detractors, among both fans and other pros. Nobody's ever complained to my face, but professional fishing is a tight, gossipy circle, so I hear things. I know some people gripe. I think it's because those people resent what I represent: change. There are so many differences between my personality and what's "normal" for an angler. I make a lot of noise. I'm confident. I'm a promoter. That builds resentment. Skeet and Ish have told me they've heard pros bitch about me. My buddy Rob has told me about all kinds of junk about me on the web. The good news is that more of it seems to be about the *way* I am than *who* I am, my approach rather than my heart. And who knows, a lot of these feelings could be in my head. But I've sensed resistance my entire fishing career.

Sometimes I wonder what steps I could take to break the ice. On that ride back to New Jersey from Louisiana, when Pete, John, and I were brainstorming on how to capitalize on my Classic win, we talked about ramping up my efforts in P.R. Making sure every interview reflects the guy I am inside, so people get a better picture of the real me. Making sure it's clear in every interview that I respect the guys who paved my road to success. Going out of my way to get to know the other anglers on tour, so they understand that all the screaming and yelling is no act. That's just me expressing my love for fishing. It isn't always easy. In a tournament situation, where time is so precious, there's no time to spark up twenty-minute conversations. And competition itself sometimes makes things difficult, too. The moment I hit the water, it's me vs. the fish. But once that day's over, I'm not the same competitive person. Game face is for game day, but when that day is done and I'm out having dinner, it's not competition anymore. I don't think a lot of people understand that distinction. Maybe some anglers confuse my aggressiveness on the water as a personal thing. The endless clips of me screaming and breakdancing at the Classic probably don't help those guys understand me any better, either. But that stuff makes me who I am and I'm not about to change.

38 LOOKING AHEAD

So that's it. That's my life. My path from New Jersey hip-hopper to bass fishing star. All the things that have made me the guy I am today. An incredible family, amazing kids, a lot of luck with even more hard work mixed in. Since the instant I pulled my first bass out of the water, in my soul I've always been a bass fisherman. I've been blessed with success, and I feel like I've emerged during an amazing time for fishing. We've got a chance to be the next big thing, to bring this incredible sport to the mainstream. That's what I'm here to do. And hey, if how I do it bugs some people, there's not much I can do about it.

There's the yin and the yang. The blessing and the curse. Everything in life has always been that way for me. The sport I love to death, my life and my passion, has caused a lot of the failures in my life, starting with my marriage. That's life, unfortunately. That's just the way it is. But the joy fishing has brought me outweighs that pain by a long shot. And that's the bottom line. The good cancels out the bad, and there's nothing in the world I'd rather do. Simply put, I'm the luckiest guy in the world.

ACKNOWLEDGMENTS

There are so many thank-yous to go around. Where do I start? Well, here's my best shot at it:

To my two girls, Drew and Rylie. You are the best thing that ever happened in my life. Thanks for being two very special little ladies. And thanks for keeping me feeling young and grounded.

To my mom. Everything I am today is because of you. You are the whole reason I strive to be the best I can be in everything I do. Thanks for all the sacrifices and commitments you made for me. I'll never be able to repay you. Thanks for being an awesome mom!

To Uncle Don. Thanks for being my mentor, friend, and favorite fishing partner. Thanks for always pushing me and teaching me to never give up. You are my number one hero.

To Gram and Pop. You are the best two grandparents in the whole wide world. Thanks for passing down the love for fishing. My Pocono memories will live forever.

To my fans. Without your support, belief, and positive energy I wouldn't have the drive and desire to succeed. With your help, we're going to take the sport of fishing to a whole new level.

To my close friends. First, to John McGraw, for being one of my best friends in the world. Thanks for believing in me and sticking with me even through the bad times. You truly are the fastest man on campus. To Pete

Gluszek for being the best friend and traveling partner a fisherman could have. To Chris Arnold and Grand Productions, keep the dream alive, brother. And finally to Amanda, you're an amazing girl!

To Andrew and Brian Kamenetzky. You did an amazing job. Thanks for putting up with my motor mouth and doing a super job of capturing my voice. Also thanks for omitting the part about Clara Barton.

Thanks to Marc Gerald and everyone at The Agency Group. Marc, thanks for believing in me from the first time we met.

Special thanks to Danielle Perez, Irwyn Applebaum, and everyone at Bantam Dell for making the process of writing and compiling this book so enjoyable.

To all of the Top Rod Bassmaster club members, especially Brian Stockl, Dave Brodzek, Chris Dalfonso, John McGraw, Bert Huffman, Big John Miltichnoski, Rick Mitchniski, Dave Jr. and Dave Sr., Timmy Fitzgerald, John Mangino, Brian MacLearn, Rich Plotkins, Don Polsco, Rob Towey, and especially to our official lost member, Steve Pellegrino, thanks for the membership dues, man.

Special thanks to Kevin Krause for driving for me and putting up with my crap. Welcome to the fish camp.

A very special thanks to my good buddy Janet Bell. Thanks for lending an ear and great advice.

To the "ugly clan" and all of my fishing bros, especially Bob Soley (suck it), Tim Roach (my xxxx is huge), Dave Mansue (cop), Marcel Venstra (cantaloupe), Jeff Hippert, Mark Schafer, Eric "Woody" Woodward, Tom Hrynyshyn, Timmy Baumen, Mitch Person, and Ted Soley.

To the old Dick's Sporting Goods lodge clan from store 82 in Mt. Laurel, including Ed Nailor, Ken Klodnicki, Geoff Cummings, and Mike Biaggi. Crank calls rule.

Thanks to BASS and FLW for bringing the sport to all-new levels.

To Ray Scott, the father of competitive fishing. Thanks for having the vision and dream. Without you there would be no pro angling.

To Forrest and Nina Wood for having the desire and drive to help create the modern bass boat and bass fishing as we know it today.

To the entire NJ BASS Federation for giving me the outlet to start my career. Except the jerk who pulled out my keys at the Delaware River.

Special thanks to all of my current sponsors. Thanks to Ranger Boats, Yamaha Outboards, Dick's Sporting Goods, Pure Fishing and the Berkley Brand of line and baits, Team Daiwa Rods and Reels, Tru–Tungsten Weights, and Mare Marine Inc.

Thanks to Octagon, especially Mark, Chris, and Giff. Let's do this, guys.

Thanks to Jason at Ocular Box studios for creating a great new web site. Also to Rob Muller for the early support.

To all the service-crew guys who put up with all our crap day in and day out. Especially Ron and Parnell at Ranger, Chad Smith and Art at Yamaha, Mike and Wilson Frazier at Lowrance, Terry Heist and Jay at Mercury, Joe Smith at Motorguide, and Andy at Triton.

To my west side homies: Bret Hite (party with the big kid), the bachelor Byron Velvick, Big Papa John Murray, Ish Monroe (Waz Up?), Travis Kline (aka the closer), "Uncle Freddy" Fred Romanas, Big Daddy Art Berry, Jack Gatledge, RJ Bennet, Aaron Martin, and Skeet Reese. Skeet, you are the originator of male stripper dancing.

To all of my peers and the other pro anglers. Especially KVD, G Money, KJ, T.O., Stone Cold, Hack Attack, Rick Clunn, Denny and Chad Brauer, Gary Kline, Jay Yelas, Guido and Dion Hibdon, Larry Nixon, Randy Howell, Scott Scuggs, Terry Baksay, Lee Baily, Paul Ellis, Joe Thomas, Rich Tauber, Alton Jones, Terry Scroggins, Woo and Chris Daves, Kevin Worth, Frank Scalish, Mark Davis, Zell Rowland, Shaw Grisby, and Kota Kiriyama.

To all of the fishing photographers, including Gerald Crawford, Charles Beck, Oga, and Seigo Saito. Your images are amazing!

To all of the fishing publications, especially *Bassmasters, BASS Times, Bass Fishing, Bassin', Bass West, In–Fisherman,* and *Field and Stream.*

To all the outdoor writers, especially Tim Tucker, Louie Stout, Vic Attardo, Don Wirth, Dave Precht, James Hall, Ralph Knisel, Curt Bobzin, Mike Jones, Robert Montgomery, Oliver Shipero, David Hart, Dan Black, and Rob Newell.

Thanks to everyone at JM Productions, including Jerry, Mike, Angie, Bowman, Marty, and all of the camera guys.

Thanks to everyone at Winnercomm Productions. Citgo Classic Adventure rules.

Thanks to all the fishing web sites, especially to Bass Fan (Jay Kumar, Terry Brown, and Jon Storm).

Thanks to Gary White and the Bassmaster University program. Awesome seminars. I hope to be a part of them for years to come.

Special thanks to Javier and Sedalia Galiana for their amazing hospitality during the Euro Cup International Bass Competition. Javier, you are the Spanish Ray Scott.

Thanks to all my schoolteachers over the years (Bingham, Voltz, Triton, CCC, and Rowan).

To Joyce Ashenbrenner and the Jimmy V Foundation. Thanks for letting me be a part of a great cause.

Special thanks to my lawyer, Dean Buono.

Thanks to Todd and Mary at Gemini Sports Marketing for the awesome designs.

To my tat shops in Jersey, Sick Creations and Mystic Eye: you guys are true artists.

Also a big thanks to the following: Sammy Lee, Bob Cobb, Fish Fishburn, Randy Hopper, Bill Dance, Hank Parker, Roland Martin, Jimmy Houston, Dee Thomas, Erwin Jacobs, Earl Bentz, John Hoagland, George McNeilly, Elizabeth Land, Dean Kessel, Christine Godleski, Stacy Twiggs, Don Cochran, Mark Zona, Tray Reed, Dave Washburn, Bill Liston, Jason Kline, Bob Steckler, Brian Blank, Gene Ellison and the Commonwealth Financial Network, Bob at Morgenstern and Associates, Mike Pallozzi at Total Planning Management, Dave Simmons, Kim Ott, Eric Naig, Dan Vesuvio, Mike McPherson, Lanny Deal, Frank Olrich, Lance Peck, Brian Lancaster, Bob Smith, Randy Pop, Ron Enslin, Preston and Anna Jickling "sorry it didn't work out," Ed Cowan, Rich Schinderite, Tony Going, Mike Kosa, George Hutchison, SJ Bass Club Association, American Bass Association, Interstate Bassin, Cox Marketing, Adam Stern, Rafael

Estrella, Deion Sanders, Greg Waldron, Walt Disney World Resort, ESPN, Fox Sports Net, Firelight, Mike and Scott at Auten Interactive, The Walker Agency, Reel in the Outdoors, The NJ Fishing Show, Bob Murray, The Main Street Pub, Auto Lenders, The Philly Diner, Waffle House, Pro Fitness Gym, Bernard's Hair Salon, Totem Lodge and Resort, Kissimmee St. Cloud, Suburban Audio and Radio, IKEA, Shane Mayfield, Todd Brown, To Bama "glass tables rule," Dennis Tubbs, Terry Seagraves, Neil and Brian Brooks, Tommy Gillian, John Delacamra, Scott Lemon, Marty Klapa, Bruce Neil, Peaches, Bob Mathews, Eric Pens, Ray Rumph, John "skelator" Carter, The Runnemede Boys (wee man, Bellows, Chuckles, Smite, Flynn, Dube, Jeff, Brud), The Rhombus Chorus, The Unique Rockers and DGC Breakers (Gregg and Rick Comb, Bill Graves aka buckshot, Shawn, Vinny and Mike D, Dave Wilson, Ronny P, Froggy Oggy), The Baseline DJ's, Emmanuel Fefis and T.W.O., Tansboro Deck Hockey (mad props to the Ball Hogs), and all the Philadelphia sports teams (go Eagles).

Special gear thanks to: Chevy Trucks, Cadillac Trucks, Givioni Rims, Perrelli Tires, Alpine Stereo, ML Audio, X-Box, Technics 1200's, M Box, Sony, Apple, Compaq, Hewlett–Packard, Brother, PalmOne, Puma, Adidas, DC Shoe Co., Nike, Converse, Under Armour, Columbia Sports Wear, Dickies Brand, Etnies, Zoo York, Split, Fox Gear, Dolce and Gabbana, Armani, Prada, Cavalli, Louis Vuitton, Gucci, Hugo Boss, Burberry, Sobe Energy Drinks and the Pepsi Co., Kellogg, Yuengling Lager, Grey Goose and Turi Vodka, Citgo, Anheuser-Busch, GT Bikes, Easton, Bauer Hockey, and MYL.

To the entire hip hop movement and all the real dj's out there. Also to the Def Tones, Tap Root, Korn, Tool, Disturbed, Rage Against the Machine, and Slip Knot for your motivational inspiration.

And finally, thanks to my own company, Professional Edge Fishing. For more information on me and products that I offer, please visit my web site at www.mikeiaconelli.com.

MIKE IACONELLI won the 2003 Bassmaster Classic. In only five years of professional fishing, he has won four majors and earned close to a million dollars. He's been fishing regularly since he was two years old. His list of sponsors includes Ranger Boats, Yamaha Outboards, Dick's Sporting Goods, Team Daiwa Rods and Reels, Berkley Fishing Line, Berkley Baits, Lowrance Electronics, and Tru-Tungsten Fishing Weights. He lives in New Jersey. Visit his web site at www.mikeiaconelli.com.

ANDREW AND BRIAN KAMENETZKY are screenwriters and frequent contributors to a variety of magazines and web sites, including *ESPN The Magazine,* ESPN.com, and *Blender*. They both live in Los Angeles.